HOLINESS

FOR ORDINARY PEOPLE

HOLINESS
FOR ORDINARY PEOPLE

Keith Drury

wesleyan
PUBLISHING HOUSE
wphstore.com
Indianapolis, Indiana

Wesleyan Publishing House, Indianapolis 46250
© 1983, 1994, 2004, 2009 by Wesleyan Publishing House
All rights reserved.
Printed in the United States of America
ISBN: 978-0-89827-403-5
ISBN (e-book): 978-0-89827-607-7

The Library of Congress has catalogued a previous edition as follows:

Drury, Keith W.
    Holiness for ordinary people / Keith Drury.
        p. cm.
    Originally published: Marion, Ind. : Wesleyan Pub. House, c1983, in series:
    Aldersgate doctrinal series.
    ISBN 0-89827-278-5 (pbk.)
    1. Holiness—Christianity. 2. Sanctification—Christianity. I. Title.
BT767.D78 2004
234'.8—dc22   2003027832

All Scripture quotations, unless otherwise indicated, are taken from the HOLY
BIBLE, NEW INTERNATIONAL VERSION®. NIV®. Copyright © 1973, 1978, 1984 by
International Bible Society. Used by permission of Zondervan. All rights reserved.

Dedicated to—
my father
Leonard Drury
who lived a life of holiness
where it's hardest . . . at home.

CONTENTS

PREFACE TO THE TWENTY-FIFTH ANNIVERSARY EDITION

Twenty-five years ago a committee of cooperating denominations—Nazarene, Free Methodist, and Wesleyan—invited me to write this book. Their charge was to explain the doctrine of entire sanctification to an emerging generation. A related goal of theirs was to place entire sanctification in a larger context of the progressive work of sanctification, both preceding and following the crisis work of entire sanctification.

Ten years later the book was still circulating and by then there was an audience outside traditional holiness churches. That led to the second edition of the book, revised with broader terminology and including a new chapter with testimonies.

Now, twenty-five years after the first edition, I am offering the third edition of this book for a whole new audience: those who have never even heard of the experience or those who have heard but doubt such an experience is even possible. Thus, this edition assumes a different tone and style and includes five completely new chapters.

I pray that this edition will continue to inspire seekers of holiness—Christians who hunger and thirst for righteousness and want to love God and others with a whole heart and will seek God's filling with love *until they find it.*

—Keith W. Drury
January, 2009

PREFACE TO THE
SECOND EDITION (2004)

When this book was first published, I expected it to last awhile and then vanish into the mist that envelops most books after a few years. That has not been the case with this book. It still has a brisk demand after twenty years. I am both delighted and surprised at its ongoing popularity. Perhaps its continued usefulness tells us more about the subject than about the author—and that we're in need of men and women to be living examples of what it means to be a fully devoted follower of Jesus Christ.

The book was originally written for young adults in the so-called holiness denominations to help them understand the teachings on holiness as taught by John Wesley and the Methodists; however, the book quickly leapt beyond this originally intended audience. In recent years there has been a soaring interest in holiness among God's people, from Charismatics to Catholics. Holiness is no longer a proprietary doctrine of any one denomination or tradition, not that it ever truly was—it's a biblical notion. But ownership of the idea of holiness is now so broad that there is a fresh demand to address how a believer can move from initial saving faith to becoming a fully devoted follower of Christ.

Since the book's release, I've been delighted most of all by the reception of this book by the young. Newer generations are not burdened by the baggage of past errors and excesses associated with this biblical doctrine. They come to the Bible and take it at face value. Since God calls us to love him with all of our heart, soul, mind, and strength, they presume one can actually obey this command. And they hunger to know how. They want to know the process God uses to make us become what he has destined us to be. They really believe it's possible to be a fully devoted follower of Jesus Christ, just as they believe it's possible to be a fully devoted husband or wife. While younger Christians freely admit they may not perfectly exemplify that ideal, they hold to the hope that their devotion can become full. This interest among the young is perhaps the greatest reason to be optimistic about the future of the church.

I pray that this little book will continue to be a guide to the disciples seeking full devotion to their master. God does not play games with us. What he calls us to be, he provides the grace to become. We're called unto holiness by a holy God. Certainly he will do his part to make us become exactly that. This is the optimistic message of biblical holiness.

—Keith W. Drury

PREFACE TO THE FIRST EDITION

What comes to your mind when you hear the word *holiness*? Perhaps you think of some saintly, gray-haired lady, a powerful evangelist, or a dedicated missionary. But do you think of yourself? Have you ever thought *you* could be holy?

The work of God's sanctification that results in a life of holiness is for every believer. Holiness isn't reserved for a select few of God's "teacher's pets," or available only to those who live far above the ordinary humdrum of daily life. Holiness is not just for pastors, missionaries, and retired folk who "have enough time to pray all day." Holiness is for all of us. Holiness is for factory workers, housewives, office managers, company executives, teachers, college students, and young, married couples. Holiness is for ordinary people. Holiness is for all who hunger for a life of love and obedience to Christ. Holiness is for you. You may not feel holy. Or you might think, "I'm not ready for this yet," but holiness is for you too.

The book is not a study of John Wesley's teaching, though anyone familiar with Wesley's writings will recognize this book's attempt to run parallel with them. And it's not a Bible study, though it includes Bible references. Neither is this a scholarly study of the doctrine of holiness, though it's based on such studies. Rather, this book tries to present holiness in an understandable, easy-to-read, life-related manner. It's written for all those who seriously seek after Christ, but especially for younger adults. In a sense, the author serves as a "translator" of the many excellent scholarly works on holiness, placing these concepts in everyday, attainable language—it aims to be a present-day plain account of holiness and sanctification.

I present this book with the prayerful hope that you will be drawn toward Christ, hungering and thirsting for a life of total love and obedience to our loving master.

—Keith W. Drury
1982

SANCTIFICATION OVERVIEW 1

A book usually ends with a summary; this book begins with it. In this chapter you will discover where the book is headed. A question-and-answer approach was John Wesley's specialty, and was widely copied by the Methodists for explaining things. We'll use that approach to present this summary.

Q: What is holiness?

A: Holiness is loving God with all my heart, mind, soul, and strength, and loving my neighbor as myself. Simply put, holiness is Christlikeness. Holiness is not an "it" as in "have you got it?" It's him

I need. In him I find purity, power, and obedience. Jesus Christ himself is the definition of holiness and its living example. He loved his Father and his neighbor perfectly. Obedience springs from love, thus holiness is perfect love.

Q: Isn't holiness only a goal for all Christians to pursue— one we can't actually achieve?

A: True, holiness is a goal, but it's an attainable goal, at least in motive and desire. Holiness is not some pie-in-the-sky, impossible dream. In fact, God commands us to be perfect—as he himself is perfect. So whatever practical holiness means, it must be possible. What kind of father would demand something of his children that was impossible? God calls us to holiness, and then helps us become holy.

The holiness message is thus optimism in God's grace—it's possibility thinking applied to spiritual formation. This is why people chained by today's pessimistic worldview have such a hard time with the idea. Modernists are in a negative mood. The proclamation of holiness marches into the midst of our pessimistic age announcing, "You can love God with all of your heart, soul, mind, being, and strength and love your neighbor as yourself."

Modernists answer, "I doubt it."

Complete faithfulness to God is the goal of all believers, but it's an attainable goal. Just as I can be fully and completely faithful to my spouse, I can be completely faithful to God. Holiness may not be average, but it's possible. With God, all things are possible. God commands us to be holy and he provides the grace to make us be what he calls us to be. God does not give impossible commands.

Q: How, then, do we become holy?

A: We become holy (Christlike) through sanctification. Sanctification describes everything God does in us to make us more like Christ. Thus our sanctification begins at conversion, progresses as we grow in grace, leads us to the point of entire sanctification, and continues beyond that until we die. In sanctification, God works in my mind, soul, spirit, and body as he changes and renews my desires, thoughts, interests, attitudes, and behaviors. Sanctification is how God transforms us into Christlikeness. Given our cooperation, we can become all that God calls us to be.

Q: When does sanctification begin?

A: Sanctification began the moment we became Christians. Since sanctification is all of God's inner work transforming us into Christlikeness, it has already begun. For most of us, the greatest leap toward Christlikeness happened at conversion. This first leap in our sanctification is called *initial sanctification*. It happened when we were born again.

Q: Why would we need anything more than conversion?

A: We need more of Christ, and God needs more of us. God, who has begun a good work in us, wants to continue it to completion (Phil. 1:6). In order to complete his work, God continues to perform a gradual sanctification in us day by day, making us more like Jesus. He draws us steadily toward right thoughts, attitudes, values, associations, and activities.

Yet all too soon, many of us discovered that our old drives and desires were not completely gone. We found a craving inside for some of the activities, thoughts, and attitudes of our old life and thus we were defeated from time to time. We began to struggle. Usually, we sided with our new desire; but occasionally—perhaps even often—we voted with our old desire and found ourselves saying, doing, or thinking things that were wrong. We were frustrated, felt guilty, and then repented and promised to do better.

Most of us who have been Christians for a while have experienced this stage of part-time victory. Many of you are living this way now. Perhaps you've never heard of any other way to live. Christians at this stage experience progress, though at times it's painfully slow.

They "win some and lose some" in obeying God. But as they gradually yield to God, they will get victory in at least these particular areas. When large blocks of time are examined, say a year or more, they can see that gradual spiritual growth is occurring. What's happening? We're experiencing *progressive sanctification*—God's gradual work in our lives, bringing our thoughts, values, attitudes, habits, and activities into conformity with Christ. Our leap toward Christlikeness at conversion, or initial sanctification, did not end our need to grow. As time passes, we continue to experience a gradual work of sanctification we call "progressive sanctification."

Q: Don't most average Christians struggle like this all their lives?

A: Yes, many, or maybe even most believers do—even in the so-called holiness churches. But even if this kind of struggle is average, there is still a better way to live. The average marriage may be poor, but a good marriage is still possible. The Bible calls us to more than average living. We're called to "walk as Jesus walked" in word, thought, and deed.

If you continually consecrate areas of your life to God, you will grow in grace and gradually gain victory. You may reach a time where there is a long period of peace and sustained obedience. It might seem like the old nature has been smothered to death. But then—just when you figured you had it beat—the old sinful nature roars back into control. There is another nature inside that is at war with our new nature. Many believers struggle like this for years or even all their lives. But it doesn't have to be that way.

Scripture teaches us that God can, with our cooperation, shorten his work and accomplish in a moment (or a very short time) what may normally be the work of many years. We call this shortening of God's work *entire sanctification*. It produces a time warp in our spiritual progress.

Q: Most Christians understand initial sanctification and progressive sanctification. But what does it mean to be entirely sanctified?

A: After months or years of progressive growth, you'll probably come to a new place—a point of decision. What is this decision? The decision is whether or not to go on. You now know that God wants everything (all of your life) offered to him as a living sacrifice. God wants your thoughts, time, talents, future, money, associations, hopes, possessions, reputation, habits, likes, and actions—everything! Give him an inch and he'll ask for a mile! You can no longer hold back a secret sin, a prized possession, or a secret habit of attitude or action. God wants to enter even these private places where you have posted "no trespassing" signs. God wants to hear, "I'm yours, Lord—everything I am, everything I've got. I'm yours, Lord." He wants you to say, "I surrender all." When we come to this point in our Christian growth, we realize we must either go on to holiness or become stagnate. If you have sensed this call, it's God calling you to complete consecration.

If you're sick of part-time victory and have a sense that there is hope, you may be ready for entire sanctification. If so, what should you do? You should do what you're hungering to do: place everything into God's hands, making a complete consecration of "all to Jesus." You hold nothing back. This is total consecration—a once-and-for-all giving of self to God. Could you decide to completely surrender all, whatever the cost? Would you be willing to go anywhere, say anything, and do whatever God wants no matter what people think? Do you want to be 100 percent committed to Jesus Christ as Lord? Would you be willing to make your daily prayer be, "Not my will, but Thine be done." If so, you're ready for complete consecration.

If you do this—and really mean it—what does God do? He accepts it. God is in the business of accepting offerings consecrated to him. If you put your all on the altar, God will accept your gift. And what will God do with a totally consecrated man or woman? God will fill you completely with his Holy Spirit. Even if he doesn't do it right away, sooner or later—if you surrender all—God will perform a major spiritual miracle inside you. He will cleanse and empower you through the Holy Spirit, enabling you to live a holy life. He will fill you with his love—for himself and others. This is *entire sanctification*: God completely and entirely filling you with his Spirit so that he fills your whole life.

How will you know? You'll notice the love that fills your heart—love for God and others. The consuming passion of your life will be to obey Christ because you love him so much—a love that came from him. You'll have a dominating hunger and thirst for holiness. Your drive to disobey will evaporate. Your heart will be filled with a fresh baptism of love. Since obedience springs from love, you will be able to obey God as much as you love him. Sure, you will still face temptation. Even Jesus Christ faced temptation. But your will is set and you're filled with love. While your performance may continue to be less than perfect, your heart can be perfect. Your battle of conflicting desires can end.

When you've experienced this second work of God's grace, you have power for service. You will be used by God in new and more powerful ways. After all, God's plan isn't to bottle you up and place you on the shelf as a holy exhibit to be admired by others. God wants to use you in his work. Entire sanctification is for service, not for show. The path to holiness always leads back into the world and God's kingdom work there. What is God's work in the world? Bringing sinners to repentance, helping believers grow in grace, and establishing Christ's kingdom on earth. This is what entire sanctification enables—God's work in the world.

It sounds impossible doesn't it? Most of us think half-hearted Christianity and part-time victory is as good as it gets. But it gets better than that. God promises so. God is in the transforming business. Maybe he can transform us sooner than we think he can. This is the impossible dream that's possible. God is a God of possible impossibilities.

Q: What happens if a person comes to this point and decides not to go on?

A: The chance will likely come again, but sometimes not for a long time. But don't think that you must decide this very minute. Most people who have experienced this level of Spirit-filling have done so after a long period of searching, thinking, studying, and seeking. The call does not drop out of the sky with a fifteen-minute expiration notice. Perhaps it would be better to call this decision point a decision period. There is time to seek. But we dare not be casual about such a matter. We're dealing with a command of God: "Be holy, for I am holy." So we should not take his commands lightly. The good news is that God's commands always come with God's grace enabling us to be what he calls us to be.

Q: Does an entirely sanctified believer have any room for improvement?

A: By all means! If your heart is entirely full of a God-given love and a dominating desire to please Christ, shouldn't you grow more? While premeditated sin may disappear in a moment, there are a hundred other ways to grow. You may be merciful, yet you can become more merciful. You may be compassionate, yet you can become more compassionate. Take marriage for example: it's possible to be completely and totally in love yet still become a better spouse. Perfect love is different than perfect performance. We can be 100 percent full of love for God, yet there is room to become more like Christ. Is there progress after entire sanctification? You can count on it!

Q: If an entirely sanctified person has a single-minded desire to please Christ, how could this person ever be tempted again?

A: Jesus was completely full of the Holy Spirit yet was tempted. There is no state of grace that puts us out of reach of temptation. Jesus Christ was tempted in every point like we are, but he withstood temptation and remained without sin. This is what he can enable us to do. We will still be tempted, for sure, but we can resist temptation just like he did.

Q: If temptation is possible, then is it possible for a sanctified person to sin?

A: Yes. There is no level of spiritual maturity from which it is impossible to fall into sin. Consider these two statements:

1. It is not possible to sin.
2. It is possible to not sin.

The first is false but the second is true. It is not impossible to sin, but it is possible to not sin. Some ask, "How long can an entirely sanctified person go without sinning?" This is sort of like asking the question "How many angels can dance on the head of a pin?" It misses the point. The point is that Jesus came to earth to save us from sin. Christ came, not just to forgive sins, but to deliver us from sinning. Can you imagine people loving God so much that they could go one full hour without purposely disobeying Christ? Most of us can. Can you imagine a whole day without purposeful sin? A week? If you can imagine these things, then you already accept the idea of holiness. All that remains is to discuss how long God can deliver his children from willful disobedience.

However, we must understand that we're dealing with sin strictly speaking. That is, when we say a sinless life is possible, we're speaking of premeditated or purposeful sin. Sometimes it's called *willful sin*. We're not saying that a Spirit-filled person can be free from sin generally speaking—the sort of sin that is falling short of the perfect standard of Jesus Christ. Entire sanctification does not produce absolute perfection but a perfection of love. We can be saved from sin strictly speaking (purposeful, known, premeditated disobedience) though we might still fall short of absolute perfection in a hundred ways. Again, consider a married couple. A husband might be completely and wholly in love with his wife and totally free of infidelity, yet he will still fall short of the perfect standard of "husband-hood." We can be free of purposeful unfaithfulness to God, yet still be less than an absolute perfect copy of Christ.

An example of perfect love may help. After several hours of hard work in his hot garden, a father glanced up to see his two-year-old toddling toward him with a glass of water. The father takes the glass, examines the smudgy fingerprints on it, and then takes a sip. The water is tepid tap water. But when he looks down at his son, he sees him gazing up at him in admiration and absolute devotion. What will the father do? The good father will gulp down the water and thank his son for "bringing Daddy that perfect glass of water." This boy's deed has fallen short of the perfect standard of ice water but the boy has completely fulfilled the royal law of love. His act was a perfect act because it sprang from perfect love. The boy is blameless.

Any falling short of the perfect standard of Christ requires God's grace and forgiveness. But we need not call this sin, strictly speaking, when the motive is pure love. Perfection in love is separate from maturity. Much of the service we offer to Christ is like that smudgy glass of tap water; it falls short of absolute perfection. Yet our heavenly Father looks into our devoted eyes of adoration and pronounces our works blameless. This is the kind of perfection God promises: a perfection of love.

The real issue here is not, "Can an entirely sanctified or Spirit-filled person sin?" but "Can such a person live above purposeful sin?" If we can, we should. The answer is that, yes, a sanctified person could sin, but we need not sin.

Q: Where are the real-life examples of this kind of life?

A: They're all around you. Whom would you nominate as the most loving person you know? In just about every church of every denomination in every country, you will find people who have totally committed themselves to God and have been filled with love.

Spirit-filled, sanctified people are not likely to brag about holiness. In fact, they may be embarrassed if you tell them how holy you think they are. Sure, these saints are often older folk, but it need not be. A multitude of young folk have been perfected in love. So don't limit your search to the elderly or to those who advertise their holiness. Search among people living in the daily trenches of life, who possess a pure love for God and others. They've experienced exactly what we've been talking about.

In fact, a person who possesses perfect love may not even understand everything you've been reading in this book. Maybe you're such a person? Many who have never had all this explained to them have experienced just what we're speaking about. When they read a book like this they say, "Yes! That's exactly what happened to me."

But maybe you cannot name a single person that you think lives like this. If so, then the ultimate answer to this question is: Jesus Christ is such an example. Jesus was born a totally human person like you and me. He was tempted in all points as we are, but he was without sin. Perhaps you say, "But that's not fair, Jesus was *God!*" Yes, he was very God but he was also 100 percent human. When tempted he never used power that is unavailable to you or me. Jesus Christ lived a holy life by the power of the Holy Spirit and loved the same way we can. This is why he lived on earth. He could have been killed as a two-year-old child in Bethlehem and functioned as our sacrifice for sin. But he lived into his thirties and showed us how humans can live with perfect love. If you've never met a real-life example of holiness, meet Jesus. He is our real-life human example of perfect love.

Q: How could I know that I am entirely sanctified?

A: First, *I can examine my love for God.* Is it entirely and completely magnetized toward Jesus Christ? Do I love God with all of my heart, mind, soul, and strength?

Second, *I can examine my love for others.* Does my heart well up with love for people: those who are unfriendly or unkind; the poor, helpless, and needy; those without Jesus Christ; even my enemies? Do I love and care for others as much as I love and care for myself?

Third, *have I totally consecrated my all to Jesus?* Is there anything I am holding back? Does God have all of my time, talents, money, possessions, future, reputation, and family—every bit of me?

Fourth, *am I experiencing power over sin?* Have I received power from God to resist all willful sin? Do I live in total obedience to Christ, with no premeditated, purposeful sin in my life?

Fifth, *has the Holy Spirit witnessed to me—inside me—that he has performed this work?* This witness may not have been clear at first, and it may sometimes be stronger and at other times fainter, but do I know it's done?

These are the indicators that combine to give me enough evidence that I can, with assurance, say that God has indeed entirely sanctified me.

Q: What is a summary of the essentials of entire sanctification?

A: These ten points include the most important ideas:

1. Holiness is perfect love—loving God with all my heart, soul, mind, and strength, and loving my neighbor as myself.
2. Holiness comes through sanctification. At conversion we are initially sanctified and begin our walk toward full holiness, but we are urged to go on to perfection, after our conversion.
3. Entire sanctification completes the work started at conversion. In entire sanctification, God purifies the heart of the believer, filling us with perfect love and enabling us to live a life of obedience and power.
4. This entire sanctification need not be late in life. For many it does occur later, but it can also occur earlier.
5. Entire sanctification is preceded by growth. Gradual death to sin and becoming alive to righteousness is called progressive sanctification and leads us toward the experience of entire sanctification.
6. Entire sanctification is followed by growth. Growth toward the perfect standard of Jesus Christ should be even more vigorous after this baptism of love.
7. Entire sanctification is not absolute. We can be pure in motive and intention, yet our performance may still fall short of absolute perfection. Perfect love does not always mean perfect maturity. There's always room to grow.
8. Entire sanctification occurs instantaneously. Though it's preceded and followed by growth, there is a certain point (or at least a period) when the old nature dies and the heart is full of nothing but a desire to please Christ fully. It may be a big event or a small one, but there is a moment when the line is crossed, just like conversion.
9. Entire sanctification requires our consecration and faith. If we will give our all to the Lord and reach out in faith God has promised to do what he said he'd do.

10. Entire sanctification results in a life of loving service. Its purpose is not to make us feel good or to make us saintly monuments but to make us clean vessels for our master's use in establishing his kingdom on earth.

Are you a seeker after this kind of holiness?

IT'S EVERYWHERE 2

HOLINESS IN THE BIBLE

The idea of holiness is virtually everywhere in the Bible and Christian history. It's not some recent notion dreamed up by John Wesley or the holiness churches. Holiness is taught clearly in the Old and New Testaments and has continually been a concern for serious Christians through all ages and in virtually all denominations today.

The Sovereign LORD has
sworn by his holiness.
—Amos 4:2

"Do not come any
closer," God said. "Take
off your sandals, for the
place where you are
standing is holy ground."
—Ex. 3:5

Remember the Sabbath
day by keeping it holy.
—Ex. 20:8

Whatever touches any
of the flesh will become
holy.
—Lev. 6:27

I will sprinkle clean water
on you, and you will be
clean; I will cleanse you
from all your impurities
and from all your idols . . .
I will save you from all
your uncleanness.
—Ezek. 36:25, 29

And now, O Israel, what
does the LORD your God
ask of you but to fear
the LORD your God, to
walk in all his ways, to
love him, to serve the
LORD your God with all
your heart and with all
your soul.
—Deut. 10:12

THE IDEA OF HOLINESS

Holiness originates with God. He alone is perfectly holy. His holiness is such an essential part of his nature that the prophet Amos declared that God has "sworn by his holiness." God is holy, above all. All other holiness begins and ends with God. To be holy is to be godly. God is the Holy One.

However, the idea of holiness in the Bible is not limited to God. Sometimes *places* were considered holy. Moses stood on "holy ground" at the burning bush. Certain times such as the Sabbath day were to be kept holy—we're to remember and keep it holy too. The Jews celebrated other feast days as holy days or holidays.

Certain objects were considered holy such as the altar, sacrifices, and related items used in temple worship. People could also be considered holy, including the priests and Levites. In fact, the entire nation of Israel was considered a holy people. The separation and purification of holy things and people is a dominant theme of both the Old and New Testaments.

HOLINESS PROMISED

Throughout God's Word there is the promise that humans can be made holy. God's Word repeatedly emphasizes the themes of individual cleansing from all impurity, renewing our hearts in righteousness, and conforming ourselves to God's image.

In the New Testament, John the Baptist announced that a greater one was coming who would baptize with the Holy Spirit and fire, to burn away the chaff from people's hearts.

THE STANDARD OF HOLINESS

Since God is a holy God, what does he expect from his followers? A holy God calls his people to be a holy people. Moses gave various laws to the Israelites, prefaced with the command to be holy because God himself is holy. In the New Testament, Peter recalled this ideal by calling upon Christians to be holy, since the God who called us is holy. Jesus concluded his command to love our enemies by stating that we should be perfect as our heavenly Father is perfect.

The logic here is simple: (1) God is holy; (2) God called us to be like him; (3) therefore we should be holy too.

What is this holiness that God expects of his people? It's a life totally dedicated to God. That's what God always wanted for his people in the Bible and it's what he wants for us today. God expected each Israelite to fear, obey, and serve him wholeheartedly. Does he expect anything less of us? This kind of life cannot be lived in human strength, so God promises to enable what he commands. He promises a "circumcision of heart" that can enable his followers to actually love God with

I baptize you with water for repentance. But after me will come one who is more powerful than I, whose sandals I am not fit to carry. He will baptize you with the Holy Spirit and with fire. His winnowing fork is in his hand, and he will clear his threshing floor, gathering his wheat into the barn and burning up the chaff with unquenchable fire.
—Matt. 3:11–12

The LORD said to Moses, "Speak to the entire assembly of Israel and say to them: Be holy because I, the LORD your God, am holy."
—Lev. 19:1–2

But just as he who called you is holy, so be holy in all you do; for it is written: "Be holy, because I am holy."
—1 Pet. 1:15–16

Be perfect, therefore, as your heavenly Father is perfect.
—Matt. 5:48

The second is this: "Love your neighbor as yourself."
—Mark 12:31

The LORD your God will circumcise your hearts and the hearts of your descendants, so that you may love him with all your heart and with all your soul, and live.
—Deut. 30:6

But your hearts must be fully committed to the LORD our God, to live by his decrees and obey his commands, as at this time.
—1 Kings 8:61

"The most important one," answered Jesus, "is this: Hear, O Israel, the Lord our God, the Lord is one. Love the Lord your God with all your heart and with all your soul and with all your mind and with all your strength."
—Mark 12:29–30

Sanctify them by the truth; your word is truth. As you sent me into the world, I have sent them into the world. For them I sanctify myself, that they too may be truly sanctified.
—John 17:17–18

It is God's will that you should be sanctified.
—1 Thess. 4:3

all of our heart and soul and, therefore, obey God fully.

Solomon dedicated the new Temple in the presence of all Israel. He concluded his dedication by commanding the people to fully commit their hearts to God. He warned them that God would not be satisfied with partial commitment; God called for total commitment. The record of the Israelites illustrates how infrequently they achieved this complete obedience. But their failure has not altered God's call. Neither has ours. God yearns for a people committed to total and complete love of himself and others.

Jesus reinforced this high call to holiness. He made it his "most important commandment." We're called to love God with all our heart, soul, mind, and strength—our whole being—not with part and not even with most of our being. All means all. No less. And this is not an unreasonable expectation. Most spouses expect the same from their mate— 100 percent love and fidelity that excludes all competing lovers.

Then, just in case we are tempted to become holy recluses, Jesus attaches a second commandment: "Love your neighbor as yourself." These two commands, loving God and loving our neighbor, provide a clear definition of practical holiness: perfect love. Jesus summarized in the two commandments all the holiness teaching found in the Bible. God is holy. He calls us to be holy. Holiness is loving devotion to God and others. It seems impossible, but God makes the impossible possible. We can live a loving life by his power.

The most obvious call to holiness is "Be holy, because I am holy." Because we're God's and God is holy, we, too, are called to be holy. It makes sense that a father would want his child to become like him. In this case, the heavenly Father calls us to have his own nature—love.

Jesus prayed at the Last Supper that his Father would sanctify the disciples. This prayer was his closing intercession for them (and us) before he went to the cross. What was this prayer for? He prayed for a sanctification resulting in service; they were headed into a hostile world with a holy message. Jesus expected a future sanctifying work to be done in these followers that would equip them with the power and unity to work in an evil world. So he prayed that his Father would sanctify them.

All through the Epistles, the early believers were repeatedly urged to be filled with the Spirit, to "put on a new man," or to trust God to "sanctify them through and through." Paul wrote to the Christians in Thessalonica that it is God's will that they be holy. Holiness is clearly God's will for his followers. It always has been. It still is. It always will be.

Therefore do not be foolish, but understand what the Lord's will is. Do not get drunk on wine, which leads to debauchery. Instead, be filled with the Spirit.
—Eph. 5:17–18

Since we have these promises, dear friends, let us purify ourselves from everything that contaminates body and spirit, perfecting holiness out of reverence for God.
—2 Cor. 7:1

Therefore, brothers, we have an obligation—but it is not to the sinful nature, to live according to it. For if you live according to the sinful nature, you will die; but if by the Spirit you put to death the misdeeds of the body, you will live, because those who are led by the Spirit of God are sons of God.
—Rom. 8:12–14

We are glad whenever we are weak but you are strong; and our prayer is for your perfection.
—2 Cor. 13:9

Dear friends, now we are children of God, and what we will be has not yet been made known. But we know that when he appears, we shall be like him, for we shall see him as he is. Everyone who has this hope in him purifies himself, just as he is pure.

—1 John 3:2–3

Therefore let us leave the elementary teachings about Christ and go on to maturity, not laying again the foundation of repentance from acts that lead to death, and of faith in God.

—Heb. 6:1

Therefore, I urge you, brothers, in view of God's mercy, to offer your bodies as living sacrifices, holy and pleasing to God—this is your spiritual act of worship. Do not conform any longer to the pattern of this world, but be transformed by the renewing of your mind. Then you will be able to test and approve what God's will is—his good, pleasing and perfect will.

—Rom. 12:1–2

HOLINESS IS FOR BELIEVERS

Some might think that the commands to holiness in the Bible are meant for people who are not yet saved. They reason that a Christian "gets it all at once." This is partially true, but a serious reading of the Bible shows there is more. Repeatedly, the Bible writers urge Christian brothers and sisters to pursue holiness or go on to a deeper level of holy living.

Paul tells the Corinthian saints to purify themselves of everything that contaminates either the body or the spirit and to perfect holiness in their lives. These Corinthian people were already saved.

Paul reminds the brothers in Rome of their old, sinful nature. He calls them to put to death the deeds of their old nature.

John tells "children of God," who do not yet see what God is making of them, that they will be like Jesus when they see him. This exciting hope was supposed to cause these believers to purify themselves—just as he is pure.

Paul tells the Corinthian Christians that his prayer is for their *perfection*—that they will become whole, mature, and complete. He concludes with an admonition that they should aim for nothing less than—you guessed it—perfection. While the biblical idea of perfection means completeness or maturity (not *absolute* perfection), the call is still clear that he expects believers to push on for something more than they already are.

In Hebrews, the readers are scolded for being baby Christians. They are urged to leave the elementary teachings and go on to maturity and completeness in Christ.

Finally, after detailing God's faithfulness throughout eleven chapters, Paul urges the Roman believers to present their bodies as living sacrifices that are holy to God. He promises a spiritual transformation, or renewal of their minds, so that they will no longer be conformed to the patterns of this world.

These are powerful promises and they are given to Christians. There's no doubt about it. Holiness is a consistent emphasis of Scripture. In God's Word, believers—brothers, children of God, Christians—are repeatedly called to something more—to go on to holiness, full maturity, completeness, perfection.

The idea of holiness is everywhere in the Scriptures. It appears, in one form or another, more than six hundred times. It pervades both the Old and New Testaments. The standard of holiness is clear: loving God with all our hearts, minds, souls, and strength, and loving others as we love ourselves. It's not merely some distant goal we pursue with little hope of ever attaining this sort of love. It's God's will for all believers. It's a present possibility for us to have a heart full of love for God and others. The promise of holiness is for regular people like you and me. Holiness is for ordinary people.

THE HOLINESS QUEST IN HISTORY

Down through the ages, serious Christians have thought, spoken, and written much about holiness (perfect love for God and others) and sanctification (God's work in us perfecting this love). Holiness is not a recent idea or invention of a few denominations or movements. There have always been people who took God's call to holiness at face value. These people searched for the means of becoming what God called them to be. The writings of early Christians, like Clement and Ignatius, ring with the hope for deliverance from sin in this life—to actually "walk as Jesus walked."

Some early seekers of holiness figured they might find holiness through self-renunciation. These ascetics denied themselves comforts of life, isolated themselves from the world, practiced daily disciplines, and eventually created the long-lasting monastic movement among laypeople. Monasticism may be the most systematic and organized quest for holiness in history.

Their hope was that self-denial and self-discipline would produce holiness in this life. They were at least partly right. For hundreds of years, the search for holiness and piety most often led to a monastery or convent full of serious Christians bent on being all that Christ called them to be. Today we might be inclined to make light of these monks and nuns as people who seem strangely out of touch with the world. However, despite the inadequacies and limitations of both the monastic and the mystic movements, the holiness which was to be found during earlier ages was often found in these movements. We must admire these folk for their quest. They were hungry for holiness and sought to be completely full of God's love in daily life. They may have missed the route at points, but they were traveling to the right destination.

During the early 1300s, men and women like Eckhart and other members of the Brethren of the Common Life sought true piety and holiness of personal life. In the late 1300s, Thomas á Kempis wrote *Imitation of Christ*, emphasizing that personal holiness—a complete purity of intention—was possible in this life and not just in heaven. Through all this time, there remained within the Roman

Catholic Church (and more so in the Eastern churches) a strata of faithful seekers after holiness through self-renunciation and God-given sanctification. Holiness is not just a Protestant idea. Both the Roman and Eastern churches had many serious seekers for holiness—perhaps even more than today.

Like most reformers in the 1500s, Martin Luther didn't deal with the idea of deliverance from purposeful disobedience in this life. Luther's and the Reformers' battles against the Catholic Church were on another front—salvation by faith alone. But some of Luther's contemporaries, notably Schwenkfeld, Munzer, and groups like the Confessors in the Glory of Christ, emphasized the real possibility of holiness and practical piety in this life.

In the 1600s, Jeremy Taylor attempted to explain holiness as a practical possibility for the workaday world. His book, *Holy Living and Holy Dying*, brought the holiness emphasis nearer to everyday living. Holiness could be for anybody who sought it, not just for those who dedicated their lives to seeking God in monasteries or convents. Holiness was for ordinary people.

George Fox, a contemporary of Jeremy Taylor, was the father of the Quaker movement. Fox not only refused to relegate holiness and piety to a monastery but also merged it with social concern and activism, as Wesley would do a hundred years later. Holiness was a practical way of living with total dedication to God and making a difference in the ordinary daily world.

During this same time period (the 1600s), German Pietism was fathered by Philip Spener, who proclaimed the possibility of holy living for every Christian. He and his followers held small group meetings for Bible study, reading, prayer, fasting, sharing, and mutual edification.

In the 1700s, the Moravians carried on the Pietists' concern for personal holiness and spiritual discipline. The Moravians' bravery in the face of imminent death during a stormy voyage to America shook John Wesley deeply and prompted his own spiritual search that eventually resulted in his conversion and seeking full and complete sanctification.

Following their Christian conversion in the 1700s, John and Charles Wesley preached, wrote books, composed hymns, sang, and debated; and a great revival of conversions and those seeking holiness followed. Simultaneously, John Fletcher preached, and Bishops Coke and Asbury led the Methodists in America. The great Methodist movement exploded around the world, especially in the new western expansionist states of America. The Methodists emphasized the definite, practical possibility of being entirely sanctified—finding deliverance from purposeful sin by being filled with love for God and others. John Wesley's writings continue to provide a central reference point for today's "holiness people."

During the 1800s, the doctrine and experience of holiness continued to ripple through most Christian movements and denominations. The Keswick movement was organized in 1874 to "promote scriptural holiness." Colleges and holiness associations sprang up as waves of holiness revivals spread across America, Canada, and back into Europe. Special holiness camp meetings were planned to promote holiness. Denominations were organized, including the Wesleyan Methodist Connection (1843), the Free Methodist Church (1860), the Church of the Nazarene (1895), and the Pilgrim Holiness Church (1897). Baptists who had received this "second work of grace" split from their former associations and organized as Reformed Baptists, especially in Maine and the Maritime provinces of Canada.

In the 1900s, the experience of holiness continued to spread, though not without distractions and abuses. After the World War I, a spirit of pessimism dominated Americans and pervaded the thinking of many Christians, making positional holiness more attractive than an actual change in lifestyle. By the end of the twentieth century, Christians hoping for improvement in love and life relied more on pop psychology, self-help tips, or recovery programs than a miraculous act of God. Fewer folk believed God could actually make changes in a person's life instantaneously, believing instead that God had moved on to "slow-cooker" methods of sanctification.

But there is a countertrend in the church too. The emerging generations are greatly dissatisfied with a religion that makes nice people who are yet uninvolved with the needs of the world. There is evidence of an increasing emphasis on holiness in Keswick and Calvinist parachurch organizations. Young adults, fed up with the shallowness of the lukewarm life, are beginning to search for something more, even if they have a hard time finding it. Charismatic churches once sidelined by holiness people are keenly interested in the miraculous work of God in sanctification.

But all of this is about North America, where a tiny part of God's church is hiding. In the rest of the world, a totally different kind of Christianity is emerging that takes seriously the claims of the Bible and expects God to perform all kinds of instantaneous miracles including healing, exorcism, and entire sanctification. Indeed, the next wave of powerful teaching and writing on entire sanctification is likely to come from overseas.

The idea of holiness is not a pet doctrine of a few denominations. Holiness is soundly rooted in the Bible, has been sought throughout the ages of church history, and is now experiencing a revival of interest, especially outside North America. There will always be people who read God's Word and see his call to pursue holiness so that we can live a life of love. These believers simply assume that God would not command more than he would enable. Since he calls us to holiness, he must be able to provide the power to actually become what he calls us to be. Thus, these faithful followers of Christ reach out in faith to

God and seek a work of grace in their lives enabling holy living. Christ's response today is the same as it has been throughout history. Those who hunger and thirst for righteousness, he *fills*. Those who become seekers, will *find*. Those who ask, *receive*. Do you hunger? Are you a seeker? Are you asking?

SEVEN APPROACHES 3
TO HOLINESS

Holiness can be found throughout the Bible and Christian history, and it's still prevalent today in most denominations' doctrines. John Wesley, like many of the early church fathers, preached the possibility of experiencing God's power in such a way that we can live a love-filled, obedient life. He taught that through God's power we can be enabled to actually obey the two greatest commandments—loving God completely and loving our neighbor as ourselves. The terminology for this experience has

This chapter is based on a joint online paper originally co-written with Dr. Chris Bounds, September, 2003.

shifted through the years and has included Perfect Love, the Upper Room Experience, being Filled with the Spirit, Baptism with the Holy Ghost, the Deeper Life, the Higher Way, Entire Sanctification, and Holiness. The idea is taught in almost all denominations today—even though some have relegated it to the back seat. The current formulation of *holiness* is often represented in the phrase, "becoming a fully devoted follower of Jesus Christ."

> John Wesley, like many of the early church fathers, preached the possibility of experiencing God's power in such a way that we can live a love-filled, obedient life. He taught that through God's power we can be enabled to actually obey the two greatest commandments—loving God completely and loving our neighbor as ourselves.

So, is it really possible that I can become a fully devoted follower of Christ in this life? If so, how? Today's denominations offer at least seven answers to this question. This chapter attempts to describe each view. We're not necessarily trying to point out wrong and right views, but demonstrating that serious Christians usually ask the question of holiness, though their answers may vary a bit. The seven approaches described in this chapter represent the most common answers given today. They're listed from the most pessimistic (about the possibility of experiencing holiness in this life) to the most optimistic. This book tilts strongly toward the answers at the optimistic end of the spectrum, but we will try to present all of today's answers to the question of holiness in a fair manner.

1. HOLINESS OF CHRIST—NOT ME

The most pessimistic view of holiness argues that all people, including born again Christians, are so sinful at the core that we can't even become partially devoted followers of Christ in this life. We will always be so sinful that we can never be holy in practice. Those with this view suggest that Christians should constantly confess their sinfulness and trust Christ's holiness, since God has imputed or assigned Christ's righteousness to us. God counts us holy if we trust him, even though we're still sinners. When the Father looks our way, Christ is between so that the almighty can't see our sinfulness; he sees only the holiness of Christ. Christ is holy, not me. Seeking holiness in daily life is futile and might even lead to more sinfulness, like pride and boasting on my own holiness, instead of focusing on the holiness of Christ. All I can do is confess my constant sinfulness and trust the holiness of Christ.

While this view enjoys a small degree of popularity in contemporary evangelicalism, it has not historically been held by most credible and respected orthodox theologians. Some have placed Martin Luther or John Calvin in this camp because both emphasize imputed righteousness. The charge might be somewhat true of Luther. Luther's primary focus, like many reformers, was on justification by faith alone. But he addresses sanctification, too. Calvin is harder to assign to this category. However, Calvin did focus most of his attention on our objective standing before God and less on our practical sanctification.

Both Calvin and Luther were influenced by the battles they fought during the Reformation—and those battles were mostly about the role of faith and works. In a curious way, the Catholics they were battling fell more on the sanctification side of that argument. However, Calvin did add to his emphasis on *imputed righteousness* (Christ's righteousness assigned to us) a doctrine of *imparted righteousness* (actually becoming righteous). Thus Calvin does not really belong completely in this first category of "holiness of Christ, not me," but probably the second one.

But some of Calvin's theological heirs dismiss Calvin's added emphasis on the actual transformation of Christians and thus argue for this first approach to holiness. This more pessimistic view of holiness is relatively rare today, though it does exist. We who have stronger views of holiness can appreciate those who hold this view, since we like their emphasis on holiness never leading to pride or boasting and that such a life comes only by God's work, not our own "works righteousness." God and God alone should get all the glory. We never discipline ourselves into holiness; it's a work of grace from God.

2. WORTHY GOAL—IMPOSSIBLE DREAM

The second view of holiness teaches that being a fully devoted Christian is not possible in this life, but we should head that direction anyway. This view says we should trust God to deliver us increasingly from sinful thoughts, words, and deeds, and gradually to empower us in love, even though we won't ever become a fully devoted follower of Jesus Christ. We should aim high knowing that we will always miss the mark. Holiness is a worthy goal but an impossible dream. Those who teach this approach to holiness see it as a *journey* more than a *destination*. We can become more devoted but not a fully devoted follower of Jesus Christ. To them, holiness is partially possible in this life, but not fully so.

This view represents the position of most Reformed theologians. Reformed folk do not discard the call to holiness; instead, they call each Christian to pursue holiness passionately, even though it will never be fully realized short of heaven. Reformed writers and preachers do not lower the bar of holiness, but raise it. Holiness is not a casual matter to Reformed folk. They call Christians to pursue being transformed into Christ's image daily and to constantly be molded after his will. They sometimes preach holiness better than those in the Holiness movement. To them, full and complete holy living may not be possible in this life, but that gives us no excuse— we should pursue Christlikeness anyway, like a spouse should seek to be a perfect mate even though they never will become one.

This approach is often seen best in the teaching and writing of John Calvin, Reinhold Niebuhr, J. I. Packer, and Sinclair Ferguson. We in the Holiness movement generously applaud this reformed approach, for it does call people to holiness in this life. We simply think God is able to finish his work sooner than heaven.

3. A MOMENTARY EXPERIENCE— BUT UNSUSTAINABLE

The third view of holiness teaches that it is possible to become a fully devoted follower of Christ in this life—but not for long. To them, holiness is possible but cannot be sustained over the long haul. They teach that a believer might experience a day or even several weeks when he or she truly acts out of the complete love of God and neighbor, and these actions can be completely untainted by selfishness or pride. Yet this complete devotion won't last long. The old man or car-

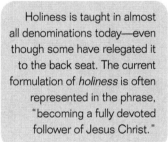

Holiness is taught in almost all denominations today—even though some have relegated it to the back seat. The current formulation of *holiness* is often represented in the phrase, "becoming a fully devoted follower of Jesus Christ."

nal nature inside us is too strong to be completely vanquished in this life. They say that inevitably these pulses of holy living will collapse, and we will return to the ordinary life of disobedience and even spiritual infidelity.

This view is held by many from the modern evangelical Lutheran perspective, as seen in the work of Gerhard Forde. Some scholars argue this was actually Martin Luther's position on holiness. Those in the Holiness movement love to interchange with those who hold this position, for we both agree that holiness is possible in this life. The only place we find disagreement is in how long one can live an obedient life. They say being holy is like walking on water—sooner or later you'll sink again. We say it can be sustained longer than you might think.

4. A SUSTAINABLE EXPERIENCE— WITH MOMENTARY LAPSES

The fourth approach to holiness teaches that we can indeed become fully devoted followers of Jesus Christ, and we can keep on being holy for a long time. Holiness can be the normal Christian life (even if it's not average). The Holy Spirit's strong enough to suppress our sinful nature so that we can live in sustained victory for months and even years. This approach is similar to the one above except for length of sustainability. It teaches that full obedient living can last a long time, just not forever. The root of sin that prompts disobedience will never be totally defeated, so even a person walking in holiness will be overtaken by sin sooner or later. Sin or disobedience is not normal, but the exception—like a car crash.

This approach is the classic understanding of holiness in Keswick theology. The Keswick movement was born in England in the mid-1800s when the American holiness revival spilled back over into England, Ireland, and Scotland. Often referred to as the "higher Christian life," this movement continues today, both inside and outside of the holiness movement, in both England and the Americas. Keswick preachers gradually distanced themselves from the Methodist preachers who taught that the carnal nature could be completely eradicated. Instead they began teaching *counteraction;*

suppression of the inner drive to sin. Columbia Bible College and Seminary in Columbia, South Carolina, was founded by one of the early leaders of the American Keswick movement, Robert C. McQuilkin. Many other holiness authors of the last fifty years have taken the Keswick approach.

Those of us in the Holiness movement are so close to Keswick doctrine that, when we read a Keswick book, we can't tell the difference. Both call people to holiness in this life and preach the optimistic possibility that we can actually live a fully and completely devoted life of love. While we differ in the nuances of doctrine, we seldom differ in our preaching. Keswick preachers don't proclaim, "You're sure to fail," but "You can live obediently."

Many holiness pastors functionally take the Keswick position when someone comes to them for counseling who has previously experienced total victory and love but has fallen back into sin. They counsel, "Get up and walk again. When you take a wrong turn you don't have to go all the way back to the beginning of the trip again." Holiness preachers and scholars love Keswick teachers, even though we believe a Christian can be victorious longer than Keswicks expect.

5. POSSIBLE— AFTER A LONG GROWTH PROCESS

The "longer way" approach to holiness proclaims that living as a fully devoted follower of Christ is a real possibility in this life, but it can be achieved only after many years of a gradual growth— putting off sin and putting on deeds of righteousness through Christ's power. This approach calls Christians to put their sin to death and move gradually closer to Christ so that eventually, usually after many years, they might become fully devoted followers of Christ. Holiness, according to this view, is to be found most among those who have been serious Christians for many years. The Christian is to follow the Spirit's leading in one area at a time until God can complete his work of sanctification—before death and heaven.

> The "longer way" approach to holiness proclaims that living as a fully devoted follower of Christ is a real possibility in this life, but it can be achieved only after many years of a gradual growth—putting off sin and putting on deeds of righteousness through Christ's power.

This view is the generally held position of The United Methodist Church—at least those who take their Methodism seriously, such as Thomas C. Oden. Those in the Holiness movement enjoy a rich relationship with those who have this view of holiness because they truly believe living a holy life is possible in this world, and they urge Christians to "go on to perfection." Chris Bounds calls this view the "longer way." Some would assign today's foremost holiness preacher Steve DeNeff to this group, though I believe he belongs in the next group, the "middle way."

6. KEEP SEEKING UNTIL YOU RECEIVE

The "middle way" approach to holiness teaches that even a young person can become a fully devoted follower of Christ and live in perfect love of God and others. Yet one cannot experience it just by asking and believing, which some call "slot-machine holiness" (just pull the lever and get holy). God sanctifies us wholly only in his own good timing, not when we ask or receive it by faith. Thus, a seeker after holiness should keep on seeking until God responds with a second work of grace that enables a life of power and purity. This approach urges Christians to keep seeking after holiness even if it takes years before God responds. This view places more emphasis on God's sanctifying than on our faith and consecration. Rather than saying "take it by faith," this approach urges Christians to "wait on the Lord" or "tarry in Jerusalem" until the Holy Spirit comes. It teaches that entire sanctification is out of our control—it's a gift of God that should be sought, not seized.

Although John Wesley's teaching is greatly debated, many scholars contend that Wesley took this view (though at other times he seems to take the next view). Many holiness camp-meeting preachers of the twentieth century took this approach in practice, when they called listeners to "come every time the altar is open until you receive

> The "middle way" approach to holiness teaches that even a young person can become a fully devoted follower of Christ and live in perfect love of God and others. Thus, a seeker after holiness should keep on seeking until God responds with a second work of grace that enables a life of power and purity.

this work of God—ask, seek, knock, and *eventually* you will get an answer; the door will be open and you will find."

7. BELIEVE AND RECEIVE BY FAITH—NOW

The last approach is the most radical. It applies "evangelism thinking" to entire sanctification. It asks, "How were you saved? Then that is how you're sanctified." You didn't have to wait until God was ready for you to be saved; rather you reached out in faith and received the gift of salvation offered to all. The same is true for sanctification; it's offered to all. This believe-receive approach optimistically teaches that any Christian of any age and level of Christian maturity can receive this full work of God by faith—just like we were saved, by asking and believing. They say, "God will not withhold any good gift from you including the filling of his Spirit—just ask and you shall receive by faith." Those with this approach offer to all the promise of "full salvation" by calling Christians to consecrate their all to God and receive by faith the second work of grace like they did the first work. Historically, this has been the most common view of the American Holiness Movement that was mothered by Phoebe Palmer and promoted through the Camp Meeting movement.

> The "shorter way" approach to holiness teaches that any Christian of any age and level of Christian maturity can receive this full work of God by faith—just like we were saved, by asking and believing. Those with this approach offer to all the promise of full salvation by calling Christians to consecrate their all to God and receive by faith the second work of faith like they did the first work.

This approach is called the "shorter way" by Chris Bounds. The holiness preachers of today tend toward the final two approaches, though there are holiness preachers and theologians who take each of the last three approaches. This book leans toward the final two approaches as well, but admires any approach that calls people to trust God's grace to change us into becoming what God calls us to be.

SO WHAT?

Do these approaches to holiness provide a multiple choice option—pick one, because they're all just as good as each other? No. The purpose of outlining these approaches to holiness is to remind us that holiness is not the pet doctrine of a few denominations who call themselves part of the "holiness movement." It's everywhere—past and present. Holiness is not an optional experience, like adding nuts to a hot fudge sundae. It's a core belief of most churches.

The final two approaches are the most optimistic and democratic approaches—holiness is for all people of any age. They are also the long-standing views of the holiness movement, though the final approach was most popular until recently. These two views do not claim the other views are false; they simply teach that God can do more than we think, sooner that we expect. While this book promotes the final two views, it respects and applauds any approach to holiness that is optimistic about the power of God to practically enable us live a daily life of obedience and love.

SANCTIFICATION AND SEX   4

*"It is God's will that you should be sanctified:
that you should avoid sexual immorality."*

—1 Thessalonians 4:3

I t is no accident that the terms *holiness* and *sanctification* often
appear closely associated with sex; both sanctification and sex
deal with the deep inner drives of a human being. Paul connected
the two in his letter to the Thessalonians by making sexual purity
a prime example of what it means to be sanctified (1 Thess. 4:3).
It's no wonder. The ancient world may have been even more
sex-crazed than our world. Sex is a good test case for trying out
the doctrine of holiness and discovering what we believe about
sanctification. Consider the story of Josh.

JOSH THE UNFAITHFUL HUSBAND—
A TEST CASE

Josh (not his real name) has been married to Julie for a decade. Their friends think Josh and Julie have a fairly solid marriage. That is, all their friends except Carl. Carl is Josh's best friend and accountability partner. The two of them meet monthly at a fast food joint to eat breakfast and hold each other accountable. Last month Carl had the wind knocked out of him when Josh confessed he had been cheating on Julie for several years.

Carl was angry at first and berated Josh for his unfaithfulness and dishonesty by never confessing this in accountability meetings. Josh's eyes gathered tears as he listened, and then he pled, "I already feel terrible about this, but I want this woman too—I want *both* women. I've tried to stop this a hundred times, but I just can't stop." Josh continued, "Is there is any hope for me? I want to be faithful, yet at the same time, I just can't break off this relationship. I don't even *want* to."

> It's no accident that the terms *holiness* and *sanctification* often appear closely associated with sex; both sanctification and sex deal with the deep inner drives of a human being.

What would you tell Josh? Doctrine can be examined as impersonal statements or argued and debated like philosophy. But a good test of any doctrine is how it plays out in real life. Let's examine how the various approaches to holiness would practically apply to Josh's sin. Ask yourself which answer you lean toward in this real-life test of the doctrine of holiness.

RESPONSE 1: SINNERS FOREVER, BUT FORGIVEN

Would you say something like this to Josh?

"Josh this is sin, but you're already forgiven of it. Christ died on the cross to forgive all your sins—past, present, and future. When you were saved, God wiped away your adultery before you ever committed it. Face it. We all sin every day, in thought, word, and deed. For you, as a Christian, your sins are gone. God cannot see your sin, for they were all removed as far as the east is from the west more than two thousand years ago on the cross. Your adultery was forgiven long ago when you trusted Christ, along with any sin you will ever commit in the future.

"You can't stop sinning because you're a sinner and saint at the same time. Saint Paul himself said he was the chief of sinners. You don't expect to do better than Saint Paul, do you? When you commit adultery, your sin simply shows the true state of your sinful nature. We are rotten to the core. Your sin should remind you of the absolute purity of Christ.

"Keep your eyes on Christ, for you are clothed with his righteousness. God can't see your sin. When he looks at you, he sees only Jesus. Christians aren't perfect—just forgiven. You can't overcome sin on earth, since holiness only comes in heaven. After all, you're human. Your job is to 'plead the blood' when you sin like this and rejoice in the forgiveness you already have."

RESPONSE 2: GRADUAL RECOVERY

Or, would you say something like this?

"Josh, what you have done is wrong, but you can eventually quit cheating on Julie. All Christians sin, and all sin is equal before God. If you break one part of the law, you're guilty of breaking the entire law. So you commit adultery, but I gossip, and other Christians cheat on their income taxes. We're all sinners and one sin is just as bad as any another. So join the rest of us recovering sinners, and we'll help each other overcome sin gradually.

"The church is not a collection of perfect people. We're a hospital for sinners who are trying to get well. As a fellow Christian, I will help you gradually overcome adultery. You might commit adultery many times for many more years, but you can reduce the frequency of unfaithfulness until at last you will have stopped altogether. When we get together, you should confess to the adultery you committed since we last met and we'll practice *spiritual breathing*—you breathe out your confession of adultery and then breathe in a fresh presence of the Holy Spirit. And, after time—maybe even a long time—you can eventually become fully faithful to your wife again. These things just take time."

RESPONSE 3: VICTORY OVER SIN
Or, perhaps you'd say something more like this?

"I understand how powerful this temptation is, but Josh, you don't have to act on these urges. You can have victory over acts of sin. You have powerful desires for this other woman, and you might have them the rest of your life. But you don't have to act on the desire. You can live victoriously. You might be an adulterer in your heart, and your mind may be powerfully attracted to this woman, but you can become a non-practicing adulterer—wanting to, but never acting on your desire. This is the victory God has for you.

"God can give you power even today to turn away from this woman and never go back again. You may still love her. You may still want her. But you do not have to act on these urges. Nobody *must* sin. It is possible to resist anything the Bible calls sin. Living above any particular sin is possible. You can leave here today by

God's power and never again cheat on your wife, even though you might still want to. Ask God today to give you the power to stop acting on your lustful desires."

RESPONSE 4: DELIVERANCE FROM INCLINATION
Or, could you go this far?

"Josh what you're doing is sin and you must stop. Go and sin no more, never again! God is offering you the power to cease your adultery. God will not let you be tempted above what you're able to resist. You're tempted to commit adultery with this woman, so you know God has already given you the power to resist that temptation. Draw on that power and stop . . . *now*!

"But there's more, Josh. God can work in your heart to change your inclination. God can deliver you! God can take away your lustful desire for this other woman. He can do this! God can fill you with love for himself and for Julie so that you won't even want to have sex with this other woman ever again. God not only can free you from the act of adultery but he can free you from *wanting* to commit adultery. He can do this—start seeking this work from God today!"

> Doctrine can be examined as impersonal statements or argued and debated like philosophy. But a good test of any doctrine is how it plays out in real life.

WHICH IS YOUR RESPONSE?

When doctrine plays out in real life we often discover our real position, no matter what we say we believe. The fourth approach is the one this book represents. It's optimistic about God's power in the life of a believer and teaches that, not only can a Christian have victory over the acts of sin, but we can even be delivered from wanting to sin.

We could have used any sin in this test of theology—lying, rage, bitterness, racism, or homosexuality. However, by using adultery, we remind ourselves of an astonishing truth: some wives believe they themselves can so enrapture a man that he will be delivered from all desire for another woman. If a woman alone might do this—how much more could *God* do it?

When God fills us with his Holy Spirit, we can become fully and completely in love with God and others.

It's the power of love. We think that if a man can love his wife fully, he can be fully faithful to her—even in his thoughts. Is this not also true of God? If we could love God fully, can't we be fully faithful to him—even in our thoughts and desires? Only God is the source of such love. Holiness is being filled with love that results in full devotion and thus full fidelity.

Of course we're dealing with a single instance of sin in the story above. The optimistic message of "holiness for ordinary people" is that we don't have to cheat on God in action or thoughts. We can be completely and fully enraptured by God, so much that we're never unfaithful again—even in our thoughts and desires. If this kind of love is possible among a married couple, why is it not possible between us and God?

It is possible. Our love for God can be perfected—not by trying, but by receiving God's filling. The Holy Spirit loves the Father and the Son completely and fully. When God fills us with his Holy Spirit, we can become fully and completely in love with God and others. Infidelity to such a person is unthinkable—not because we're fighting so successfully against sin, but because we love so completely. This kind of love can only come from God, for God is love.

SANCTIFICATION AND HEALING 5

There is a long history of connection between healing and holiness. In fact, many holiness churches followed the emphasis of the Christian and Missionary Alliance with a "four-fold gospel" (salvation, sanctification, healing, and the second coming). It's not surprising that healing and entire sanctification are related since both expect a miraculous act of God that actually changes things.

WE ARE EXPECTED TO EXPECT HEALING

Physical healing is not some wacky idea on the fringe of Christian thought; it's provided in the atonement. Much of Christ's ministry was focused on healing. Jesus called the Twelve together and gave them power and authority to heal diseases. He did the same when he sent out the seventy (Luke 9–10). After Jesus ascended into heaven, Christians continued to experience God's healing and were expected to seek healing from God. James even suggested an outline for a healing service: we're to call for the spiritually mature elders of the church to pray and anoint the sick; God would raise them up (James 5). In the ensuing two thousand years, most Christians expected God to heal and claimed he did.

The expectation for healing has fallen on hard times among progressive modern church folk today. Healing is generally considered possible, but unlikely. God could heal if he wanted, but most moderns don't expect healing, in spite of "expect a miracle" slogans. Christians today might hope for healing, or believe healing is possible, but few expect it. Though most Christians say healing is theoretically possible, they secretly doubt most reports of actual healing. Moderns have been disappointed too often to believe in actual healing. Most Christians today have developed a broader view of healing than the simple "just ask and it will happen" approach. Thus the simple believe-and-receive approach is nuanced as follows.

SOMETIMES GOD DELAYS HEALING

The first nuance to our practical healing doctrine is the reminder that God does not always raise up the sick right away. We say, "God heals but he sometimes delays his healing." We remind ourselves that our personal faith—no matter how strong—cannot force God to do something in our timing. God can and will heal, but only when God determines to do so and in his own timing. Since we believe God sometimes delays, we urge people to not give up but "keep seeking" and "wait on the Lord" for healing until he acts.

GOD SOMETIMES HEALS SLOWLY

We've also discovered that God sometimes heals gradually, not instantaneously. We say "God is healing my wife; we can see her steady progress back toward full health." While the Bible seems to suggest mostly instantaneous healing events, the healings we testify about are usually gradual. As a result, we have determined that God usually heals slowly today and not in a single moment. We now tell each other that, even if you get well slowly, it's still God who does the healing. He should be given the glory. In some sectors of the church, only gradual healing is expected and any reports of instantaneous healing are doubted.

> Physical healing is not some wacky idea on the fringe of Christian thought; it's provided in the atonement.

GOD OFTEN USES HUMAN MEANS FOR HEALING

In a modern, medical world, we have come to accept that God uses human medicine as a means of healing. We pray that God will guide the surgeon as he operates and removes the tumor. We believe that modern medicine is a gift from God to accomplish healing just like he once did miraculously. It's not that we don't believe God couldn't take a tumor away without surgery; we just believe God usually uses modern medicine to bring healing and expects us to go to the doctor when we're sick, not "just pray."

Even those among us that preach radical "faith healing" don't expect God to heal their toothaches or eyesight; they go to the dentist and get their tooth filled, or to an optometrist to get a new set of glasses. We have come to believe that God expects us to take advantage of these "natural processes" for healing and that he works through and alongside them to bring healing. When we're declared cancer-free, we pay the surgeon and give God the glory: "God guided the doctors and gave his healing through them."

GOD CAN HEAL INSTANTANEOUSLY

Most Christians today have heard at least one story of how God healed a person instantaneously. Some don't believe this is possible, but most of us believe it can happen and sometimes does. When someone testifies that "My husband went into surgery to remove the tumor and when they opened him up, the tumor was completely gone," we believe it might have really happened. We moderns hope it did happen, even if we secretly think it might have been a simple mistake on the X-rays.

We can more easily believe that such miracles happened in the past or in faraway places. When the Bible tells us that people came to Jesus with leprosy and went away clean, we nod our heads and believe it happened right away. Or, when we hear stories of how God healed someone in India or Africa, we repeat the stories or forward them by email and praise the Lord. We believe healings like this happened in the past or that they happen in other places today, even if we have seen little of such instantaneous healing in our own lives. It's just hard for us to believe they can happen to us now.

> Much of Christ's ministry was focused on healing. Jesus called the Twelve together and gave them power and authority to heal diseases. He did the same when he sent out the seventy.

GOD EVENTUALLY HEALS US COMPLETELY

The easiest kind of healing to accept is the eventual healing all Christians receive. All of us believe that once we get to heaven we will finally be completely healed. In heaven there will be no sickness, no disease, no death. In fact sometimes we say "God healed her by taking her home" when a sick woman dies. We might be fudging a bit by labeling death as healing, but we're technically right—for we shall all be whole in heaven. Even the Christians who are completely skeptical of healing reports still believe that ultimate healing will occur at death; their doubt is that it can occur here and now.

HOLINESS AND HEALING

Our view of healing and our view of holiness are remarkably similar. Consider these views of holiness using similar categories.

GOD SOMETIMES DELAYS SANCTIFICATION

While the Bible seems to promise complete cleansing "just for the asking," we have found that sometimes even a completely consecrated believer has to wait for God to cleanse and empower. So we urge people to not give up, but to keep seeking and wait on the Lord until He acts.

GOD SOMETIMES SANCTIFIES SLOWLY

Sometimes God does not sanctify a person in an instant but produces holiness gradually. In some sectors of the church, only gradual sanctification is expected. Reports of instantaneous sanctification are doubted.

GOD OFTEN USES HUMAN MEANS FOR SANCTIFICATION

In a modern, psychological world we have come to accept that God uses human counseling and prescription drugs to help humans overcome sin and dysfunction. It's not that we believe God couldn't make people pure, but we believe that God usually uses the God-inspired fields of medicine, counseling, and recovery groups to do so now. When we're freed, we pay the counselor's fee but give God the glory.

GOD CAN SANCTIFY INSTANTANEOUSLY

Here the parallel begins to break down. While many Christians today have heard at least one testimony about how God sanctified a person instantaneously, fewer believe it really happens today. They might believe that the apostle Paul or John was sanctified, but they doubt there is anyone alive who has been entirely sanctified. This is the greatest challenge preachers of entire sanctification face. If Christians believe nobody alive has ever experienced perfect love, they will not believe it could happen to them. They like the idea, and wish it could be true, but they doubt it's possible. Is this why the experience is so rarely claimed today?

EVENTUALLY GOD SANCTIFIES US COMPLETELY

This is the easiest kind of sanctification to accept—final sanctification in glorification. In a sense, everyone believes in eventual sanctification. Even the Christians who are completely skeptical of every testimony they've ever heard about entire sanctification still believe that when we see him we shall all be completely pure. The challenge is in believing that sanctification can occur here and now.

Maybe there's a connection between our view of healing and our view of holiness. We're full modernists and doubt the miraculous in both physical and spiritual healing.

HOLINESS *AS* HEALING

It is beyond the scope of this book to deal with theology and biology, but we should at least mention it here; we might see these two fields interacting more in the future. We're beginning to see some possible evidence of genetic inclinations toward certain sins. It's too early to tell, but biology might one day discover material propensities to sin, or at least some sins. Old-timers used to preach as if carnality was a substance or thing that God could remove through eradication. Modern proponents of holiness (including myself) have mocked this notion and offered models of sinfulness that present the malady as spiritual, not material. However, we might discover in the future that there are physical propensities to certain sins or even all sin that are inherited genetically.

If future biological researchers find that there is something broken in the human genetic structure that inclines humans toward sin, the connection between healing and holiness will be even more startling. Entire sanctification would then be understood as an actual *physical* healing more than a *behavioral* or *spiritual* healing. If this happens, all of us modern proponents of holiness will have to apologize to our grandparents whom we mocked!

> The expectation for healing has fallen on hard times among progressive modern church folk today. Healing is generally considered possible, but unlikely. God could heal if he wanted, but most moderns don't expect healing, in spite of "expect a miracle" slogans.

Now, don't go running off a cliff with this idea—discoveries in behavioral genetics are in their infancy. There is not nearly enough evidence to say this is true. But the emerging biological evidence appears to hint in this direction. In any case, the hope of sanctification is that we can experience complete healing from the malady we inherited, whether spiritual or physical; we can be made whole again. No matter which way or combination of ways God actually does this work, we yearn for complete and perfect love and obedience.

IMAGES OF SANCTIFICATION 6

A picture may not always be worth a thousand words, but Jesus frequently used images and illustrations to communicate. He was comfortable illustrating a heavenly meaning with an earthly story and used metaphors, parables, similes, and even an occasional allegory.

Jesus used examples from home life, including yeast spreading in the bread dough, sewing patches on old clothing, and storing new wine in old wineskins. He moved into the worlds of nature, commerce, and interpersonal relationships with equal ease, telling stories about sowing seeds, pearl merchants improving their stock, and two boys in rebellion—one who ran away, and the other who stayed home. Why did Jesus use illustrations, images, and stories? Jesus never wrote a book, not even a book in the New Testament; he was a preacher. He preached to crowds on grassy hillsides, along roadways, and in the midst of the bustle of the Temple area. His listeners had no digital recorders. They couldn't get a printed copy of Jesus' latest message or download it to their iPods. They had to *remember* what he said and images are memorable.

Jesus knew what most of us still need to learn—that people remember narratives best. Stories give us a hook on which to hang truth. They linger in our minds, reminding us of the truth long after we heard them. A story doesn't tell you what to think. It's a container for you to fill with meaning. Sometimes Jesus filled the container for us, but mostly he told the story and let the Holy Spirit supply the meaning. Think of it, his stories are still being told two thousand years later.

Of course, there are limits in using images and illustrations. Most illustrations, like the parables of Jesus, have one central truth. We might discover a wealth of other truths in a story or parable, but these must not be given full authority unless they are carefully considered in light of all other scriptural teaching. As we think about a few images and illustrations of sanctification, keep this in mind. Be careful not to make allegories out of these images, forcing every element to mean something. If taken too far, all illustrations break down. However, if we stick to the central points of the illustrations they can be extremely helpful in understanding God's sanctifying work.

THE HUMAN SACRIFICE

In our day of animal rights, the idea of animal sacrifice seems crude and inhumane. But in the ancient world, almost every religion had some form of sacrificial worship. The Jews had a particular system of sacrificial rituals. Whole chapters of the Old Testament are devoted to the exacting methodology prescribed for selecting and sacrificing a lamb, goat, or bull to God. The sacrifice was to be perfect—without any spot or blemish. The animals were brought to Jerusalem where they were offered as sacrifices for the sins of the people.

> Instead of offering a sheep or a goat, we're called to offer *ourselves*. Here is an illustration of *total consecration*. Consecration precedes sanctification. Consecration is our part; sanctification is God's part.

The Gentile readers of Paul's letters would have been familiar with the many pagan religions that also used sacrifices, in some cases including human sacrifices. So both Jewish and Gentile readers would clearly understand what Paul meant when he said:

> Therefore, I urge you, brothers, in view of God's mercy, to offer your bodies as living sacrifices, holy and pleasing to God—this is your spiritual act of worship. Do not conform any longer to the pattern of this world, but be transformed by the renewing of your mind (Rom. 12:1–2).

The apostle Paul, calling his Roman readers "brothers," urged them to "offer their bodies as living sacrifices" to God. Instead of offering a sheep or goat, we're called to offer *ourselves*. Here is an illustration of *total consecration*. Consecration precedes sanctification. Consecration is our part; sanctification is God's part. We're called to place our all on the altar. Consecration is giving God our time, talents, thoughts, money, reputation, family, hopes, dreams, and future and then climb on top of all that and give ourselves completely to God. "I surrender all."

> God can cleanse us from thoughts, words, deeds, and attitudes which are out of character with his will for us. God cleanses us, and then presents us to himself without spot or wrinkle, holy and clean.

One aspect of the work of entire sanctification is the part we do—consecration. Before God will do his perfecting work in us, we must be willing to sacrifice anything—everything—to him. God doesn't want our second best or leftovers. He wants the best we have to offer him—all of us. God does not entirely sanctify people who are interested only in a one-hour-a-week, casual religion. He does not ask for our physical death, but the death of self-centeredness. It's sacrificing our inclination to be our own boss. It's surrendering completely to the Spirit. This is a once-and-for-all sacrifice, yet a continual sacrifice—a *living* sacrifice. The image of sacrifice is about consecration.

What will God do in response to your total consecration? Paul says God will "renew your mind" so it is "transformed," empowering you to resist the world's attempts to squeeze you into its mold.

CRUCIFIXION ON A CROSS

Crucifixion was a common mode of execution during Bible times. Compared with today's standards, all forms of executions in ancient days appear cruel and unusual. Criminals would be tried, found guilty, and whisked off to their execution in a matter of hours. The crucifixion of Jesus is an example of such swift "justice." The readers of the epistles were not strangers to the idea of killing. Violent executions were common then, sometimes a thousand at once. These Christians knew what it meant to crucify or mortify a person.

> For we know that our old self was crucified with him so that the body of sin might be done away with, that we should be no longer slaves to sin (Rom. 6:6).

> For if you live according to the sinful nature, you will die; but if by the Spirit you put to death the misdeeds of the body, you will live (Rom. 8:13).

The New Testament writers often use crucifixion as an image for what Christians were called to do. They were to be self-executioners. While some Christians were actually being executed for their faith, Paul instructed the rest to crucify themselves. The hunted were to become the executioners. What were they to crucify? They were to crucify their old selves. They were to "put to death" whatever belonged to their earthly natures (Rom. 6:6; 8:13; Col. 3:5). They were to execute their old nature and the words, thoughts, and deeds which sprang from their old nature.

Kill. Mortify. Execute. These are powerful images! This picture is not about controlling, suppressing, or managing the old life—it speaks of death. A body hanging on a cross may take a while to die. It took Jesus half a day to die. But make no mistake, crucifixion is meant to be terminal: full death of the old life. What a pointed picture of the terminal work of ending the old life that sometimes survives even in the life of a Christian.

CLEANSING THROUGH WASHING

The first two images or illustrations help us understand our part in sanctification: consecration. The next two help us understand God's part in sanctification: cleansing and filling.

Paul uses a scrubbing image in connection with sanctification in his letter to the Christians in Ephesus. Right in the middle of a discussion on how a husband should treat his wife, Paul uses Christ's cleansing work as an illustration.

Husbands, love your wives, just as Christ loved the church and gave himself up for her to make her holy, cleansing her by the washing with water through the word, and to present her to himself as a radiant church, without stain or wrinkle or any other blemish, but holy and blameless (Eph. 5:25–27).

Laying aside for a moment the teaching here to husbands and wives, let's focus on Christ's sanctifying work in his church. It says:

1. Christ gave himself for us.
2. His purpose is our cleansing.
3. He does this by the "washing with water through the Word."
4. He plans to present us to himself.
5. We will be radiant, without stain or any other blemish, holy and blameless.

Sacrificial lambs arrived in Jerusalem matted with dust and dirt from their desert travel to the city. The lambs entered through a special sheep gate and were taken directly to a designated pool of water—the "sheep pool." At this pool they were thoroughly scrubbed to remove the dust or dirt from their coats. When they dried in the desert sun, they could sparkle like fresh snow. These lambs-without-blemish were now clean and ready for sacrifice. Only after this cleansing bath were they routed into the Temple to be presented on the altar as a sacrifice to the Lord.

What a striking illustration of Christ's cleansing work! His sacrifice on the cross influences far more than our initial conversion. We may be selected and fully set apart for God, yet we can gather quite a bit of travel dust on our way to the altar of complete sacrifice. Will we offer a dirty sacrifice to God? We won't. Sheep cannot wash themselves, and neither can we. We want to offer ourselves to God, but we're dirty. What can we do? We simply follow Jesus to the pool of God's grace and surrender to his work of cleansing. God will cleanse away the accumulation of worldly dust from us. If we get into God's pool, he will do the scrubbing. God can cleanse us from thoughts, words, deeds, and attitudes which are out of character with his will for us. God cleanses us, and then presents us to himself without spot or wrinkle, holy and clean. This is the cleansing work God can perform when he sanctifies us wholly. Cleansing. Purifying. Sanctifying. It happens when we get into God's pool.

There is a constant connection between sanctification and the Word of God. He will cleanse us by the washing with the Word. God's Word has cleansing power. Could it be that the reason so few people live a holy life today is because there are so few people who are regularly bathing in God's Word?

What is the agent of cleansing? His Word. There is a constant connection between sanctification and the Word of God. He will cleanse us by the washing with the Word. God's Word has cleansing power. Could it be that the reason so few people live a holy life today is because there are so few people who are regularly bathing in God's Word? Sunday school classes, small groups, women's groups, and preaching have all drifted gradually away from the Bible and chase after what are deemed to be more interesting topics. In our race to meet people's felt needs, have we failed to meet their real and deepest need?

We can be completely cleansed by Jesus Christ through his Word. He will present us to himself holy and perfect without stain. That is what God does in purifying our hearts. He will do it for you. Will you get into the pool?

SPIRITUAL DRUNKENNESS

In Ephesians 5, Paul selected perhaps the strangest image of all to illustrate being filled with the Holy Spirit. He cautioned the believers in Ephesus against becoming drunk with wine and encouraged them, instead, to be filled with the Spirit.

Is the use of drunkenness in connection with Spirit-filling accidental? Probably not. People in all cultures understand drunkenness. Everyone has seen men and women who have sold out to alcohol. Alcohol becomes the driving force of life, pushing ahead of family, friends, job, wealth, position, power, or popularity. A drunk is driven to drink. His or her thirst is unquenchable. A real drunk is not satisfied with just a sip. A drunk wants to be *filled* with alcohol. Drinking becomes the one great passion in life.

> A Spirit-filled man or woman is totally given over to pleasing God. The driving force of life is obedience to God. The thirst for holiness is unquenchable. No longer satisfied to be a sipper of the Spirit, they want to be *filled*.

When an alcoholic becomes filled with alcohol, he or she is a changed person. He or she does things totally outside normal behavior. We say he or she is "under the influence" of alcohol.

Paul's image is dramatic. Substitute Holy Spirit for alcohol, and we get a description of a Spirit-filled person. A Spirit-filled man or woman is totally given over to pleasing God. The driving force of life is obedience to God. The thirst for holiness is unquenchable. No longer satisfied to be sipper of the Spirit, they want to be *filled.* They become sold out to God, completely "under the influence" of the Holy Spirit.

Have you been content to be a social drinker of God's Spirit? If so, would you totally sell out to Christ? Would you let the Spirit fill your heart, mind, soul, and body—all of you—to the extent that you live daily life totally "under the influence" of Christ? Are you thirsty for this kind of life? "Blessed are those who hunger and thirst for righteousness, for they will be filled" (Matt. 5:6).

The first four images of sacrifice, crucifixion, scrubbing, and filling are biblical images. There are other Bible illustrations, but some not found in the Scriptures are also helpful in understanding sanctification. Consider these two examples.

THE MAGNET

Imagine holding two pieces of horseshoe-shaped metal in your hands. They look exactly alike. They are of the same weight, material, and size. You cannot tell them apart. However, after using them for a while, you discover that one of these pieces of metal has a power that the other does not. It has a special quality we call magnetism. This quality has endowed the piece of metal with a new force.

This metal is naturally attracted to certain other metals. In fact, a tiny needle empowered with this force and balanced on a point will point to magnetic north no matter where you are. The force in that tiny piece of metal gives it a new orientation it didn't have before it was magnetized.

So it is with believers who receive God's work in entire sanctification. These people experience a new force. They find themselves habitually drawn toward holiness and obedience, as a compass points north. Their desire is magnetized toward Christ. No matter where they are, their inner nature points toward righteousness.

It is not that something was taken out of the metal to make it magnetized, and in a way, nothing really was put in. Magnetizing a piece of metal is merely bringing an outside force to bear so that all the inner molecules are oriented in concert, each one aligned with the others—north one way, south the other. What a picture of what God can do in the heart of the Spirit-filled Christian! God can reorient every area of life—thoughts, words, deeds, attitudes, future, home, reputation, work, money—so they point toward Christ. Wouldn't it be wonderful if God could do this in you?

THE DEED TO MY HOME

Robert Munger in the little booklet *My Heart, Christ's Home*, gives us a fresh picture of sanctification and total surrender. Imagine for a moment that your entire life could be represented as a home. Various rooms would represent the many compartments of your life—a room for your time, another room for your talents, and still others representing your appetites, money, future, reputation, thought life, and possessions. There are also dozens of other rooms, closets, and hiding places.

Then Jesus comes along and knocks on your front door. After a period of conviction, you invite him to come into your home—you receive Christ.

But when Christ enters the front door of your life-home, he doesn't sit down in the living room to join you for a cup of tea. You may have expected Jesus to come for a visit, but you discovered he came in to clean up the house. Rather than having a cup of tea with you in the living room of your life, Jesus immediately went to work cleaning up the living room. Out went evil deeds, habits, bad language, and sinful associations from your old life. Soon there is quite a pile of trash outside the door—the sinful trash of your old life. All this time he recruits your assistance. He does the work, but you must cooperate.

Soon there is a fresh paint job in the public living area of your life and Jesus began moving in new furniture—godly language, holy concerns, and spiritual habits and associations. Within six months to a year or so, Jesus has totally renovated the public living area of your life-home. Others can tell. They see a difference. Jesus did not come into your life to drink tea. He came to renovate! This is initial sanctification—conversion.

But once the public areas were cleansed, you might figure Jesus would sit down to that cup of tea.

> Believers who receive God's work in entire sanctification find themselves habitually drawn toward holiness and obedience, as a compass points north. Their desire is magnetized toward Christ.

No. He now leads you into the kitchen, garage, dining room, bedrooms, basement, and attic and one by one, transforms each into beautifully cleansed areas. Others may not even visit these areas but Jesus renovated them with your cooperation. This is progressive sanctification.

But let's say that eventually your enthusiasm for renovation diminished. You became satisfied with the renovation so far. Yet Jesus keeps probing deeper, dealing with hidden thoughts, habits, or attitudes, some of which you quite honestly cherish. Perhaps you begin to drag your feet on the continued renovation project. You lose motivation. Maybe even start to resist his work?

Let's say at some point in this process you ease away from Jesus' side and slip into a private closet, taking with you a few of your favorite relics of your old life. You carry these secret sins into the closet and hide. You're now again on the other side of the door from Jesus.

What will Jesus do? He will find you. He will come to the closet where you're hiding and knock again. "Look, I am standing here knocking. Open up and let me in." He softly knocks. "I want *all* of you—to make you mine completely."

Can you picture struggling in the closet of final holdout? Jesus keeps on knocking, sometimes loudly, sometimes softly. Jesus is a persistent renovator. This is a second conviction. It's like the first conviction when God was on the front porch knocking, but now he's inside and he's knocking on your secret closet door.

Finally (let's hope) the irony of it all occurs to you. Why are you on the opposite side of the door from your loving master? He has already totally changed your life. Every bit of trash he has cleansed deserved to go. You're a better person for it. All those new attributes he brought in were beautiful and good. He loves you more than any other ever has. He knows what's best. You shake your head and say to yourself, "Why am I hiding in here from him? He knows more about managing homes—and lives—than I could ever imagine."

What will you do? Will you fling open the closet door? Will you place the remnants of your old life into his hands? You might do even more. Can you imagine rushing downstairs to your office and spinning the dial to your combination safe to remove the title deed to your home? Turning to Jesus, you might take out your pen and sign over the deed to your entire home to him. You place the deed in his hands, and say, "Here, take my whole home. It's yours, Lord. Everything I've got. Everything I am. I'm yours, Lord. From now on, you're the owner here. You manage this home. You direct the remodeling. You decide what must go and what will be brought in. I have signed

> This is entire consecration—giving my all to Jesus. Making him absolute master of my life—the owner. I become his assistant in the continual renovation project of my life.

everything over to you. This is your place, not mine. Do whatever you want with this home. I'll cooperate."

This is entire consecration—giving my all to Jesus. Making him absolute master of my life—the owner. I become his assistant in the continual renovation project of my life.

And what will he do? Will he finally sit down for tea and rest from his cleansing and renovation work? No! Now that he is the absolute master of your life, he will unleash the most ambitious restoration project. You may have been satisfied with a bungalow; he intends to transform your life into a mansion! This is entire sanctification and the continual sanctification that follows. As long as we have breath, his work in us is never done.

What about you? Have you been a Christian for a while and allowed him to make progressive changes in your life? Are you cooperating? Or are you hiding in the closet? Do you hear the knock? What will you do?

GROWING TOWARD ENTIRE SANCTIFICATION 7

anctification is the word used to describe everything God does in us to make us more like Christ. It's an umbrella term including the following:

Initial Sanctification—what God does at conversion to transform us.

Progressive Sanctification—God's gradual work which helps us gradually grow in grace as believers.

Entire Sanctification—God's major reorientation in us cleansing and filling us with love for God and others.

Continual Sanctification—God's continual daily cleansing of Spirit-baptized believers, constantly making us more like Christ in word, thought, deed, and attitude.

Final Sanctification—God's final transformation of us at death, completing his work and preparing us for heaven. This is also called "glorification."

All five of these aspects of sanctification are biblical. Sometimes people confuse one stage with another. In this chapter, we will deal primarily with the first two stages: (1) God's work of initial sanctification at conversion when we are saved, and (2) progressive sanctification, the gradual growth in a Christian's life, moving toward the experience of entire sanctification, the cleansing by and filling with the Holy Spirit.

This chapter is a little different. It's written in first-person style as the testimony of a woman in her mid-thirties. We'll call her Sue. Listen to her descriptions of how she experienced these first two stages of sanctification.

SUE'S STORY

SATAN'S SLAVE

"Before I was a Christian, I was really nothing more than a slave—a slave of Satan. I didn't realize it then, but I lived in regular disobedience to God even though I thought I was a pretty good person. To be honest I didn't want to stop sinning. At least I didn't want to stop committing the 'nicer' sins. I enjoyed sinning, though I didn't call it sin, because I did not know what God called sin. I figured that since I never killed anyone or did anything really bad I wasn't that much worse off than most of the religious people I knew. So, I'm not saying I admitted that I was a big sinner. I suppose I thought of myself as a little sinner . . . or maybe a medium-sized sinner. I see now that the Devil had me on a string. I lived totally for myself. My biggest sin was selfishness.

"There was this women's Bible study I attended occasionally where I wound up feeling funny. And I occasionally wondered if there was something more to life than living just for myself. Yet living for me and satisfying my own desires was what I did. I 'turned over a new leaf' occasionally, and made some New Year's resolu-

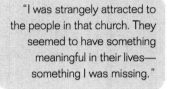

"I was strangely attracted to the people in that church. They seemed to have something meaningful in their lives— something I was missing."

tions. But these commitments usually didn't last, and I fell back into my standard pattern of self-centered living. I didn't call it selfishness then. I called it good sense.

"I don't mean to say I never did anything good. I did lots of good things. In fact, I was quite respected as a good, moral person at my office. I had heard about Jesus and about people being 'born again,' but to be quite blunt about it, I figured I was doing pretty well without that religious crutch. My belief at the time was that if everybody would just do their part, the world would be a better place. So I tried to grab all the satisfaction and joy from life that I could, while at the same time attempting to do some good things along the way for others. I was pretty satisfied with how my life was turning out.

"I thought I had life under control, but then everything began to fall apart. Little by little, everything went south. I first began to doubt whether my house, cars, family, and summer cottage really brought lasting satisfaction. At least they were not helping my marriage. I was screaming at the kids all the time and I began suspecting my husband of cheating on me. I discovered that my oldest son had been skipping school; then he was brought home by the police one night at 2:00 A.M. My life had begun to unravel."

CONVICTION

"My neighbor Janet was always bugging me to go to Bible study or church with her. I attended several Bible studies, but I didn't fit in. So I kept making excuses to her, saying that someday I was going to start, but not this week. 'Religion is good for kids, but adults shouldn't need it,' I'd say to myself. As time passed, I searched for greater meaning, something more important than living for myself. I was tired and weary at the end of every day, even tired of living for myself. I watched Janet and her family next door. They seemed to 'have it all together.' My idea of Christianity was long faces, a judgmental attitude toward others, and piles of rules to follow. Religion didn't look like fun to me. But Janet and her family were cheerful, loving, and actually seemed to be happier than our family. What was their secret? Could it be simply going to church?

"One Sunday, I woke up early. I was restless and decided I would go to church with Janet. I called her before I made coffee. I didn't realize it was 6:30 A.M. and actually I got her out of bed! But Janet was enthusiastic.

"It was a crazy morning. I was strangely attracted to the people in that church. They seemed to have something meaningful in their lives—something I was missing. They didn't seem judgmental at all. When the pastor gave the sermon, it was funny. It seemed like he was talking directly to me. I don't remember much of what he said, but I began hurting inside like I'd done something wrong. I had started to attend church so I could feel better about life, and the opposite was happening—I was feeling miserable! At the end of the service the pastor invited people to come up front to pray to become a Christian. Tears were forming in my eyes. I wanted to go up, but I didn't.

"I kept going to Janet's church almost every Sunday for the next few months. I gradually realized that they had something that was real, something I needed. Almost every Sunday the pastor invited people to come forward and pray at the end of the service. I *almost* went up every week, but I didn't. I was afraid it wouldn't work for me. There was something that held me back. I figured I just wasn't ready yet. I did begin to read a Bible Janet gave me, but it didn't make much sense. But I thought it might help me out somehow. Janet got me to start attending the Saturday morning women's Bible study so I wound up in church two hours every week! In that Bible study I heard other women tell how they became Christians or had 'been saved,' as they called it. They described the difference it made in their lives as if it was magic or something. Hearing their stories was powerful for me. These changes they talked about were the changes I needed."

> "I confessed to God that I was a sinner. I said I was more than a little sinner; I was a big sinner for living all for myself. I asked God to forgive me. I asked him to give me what these people had."

CONVERSION

"Finally one morning I could stand it no longer. When the pastor asked people to come forward I went right away. Janet went with me. I cried. Janet cried too. I confessed to God that I was a sinner. I said I was more than a little sinner; I was a big sinner for living all for myself. I asked God to forgive me. I asked him to give me what these people had.

"What a difference! It actually seemed that the whole world was brighter after church that day. My husband noticed the difference that very week. When my kids saw that I had quit yelling and cursing at them, they were mystified. My boss even noticed and said, 'You've really changed lately—for the better, I mean.' My best friends began asking, 'What happened to you? You seem different.' I didn't say anything at first but finally I told them I had become a Christian. Some said, 'I always thought you were a Christian anyway.' Others shook their heads and figured I had gone off my rocker. But one by one, they admitted that I was a nicer person since I had 'gotten religion.'

"Of course, I still faced problems. But I had new energy to tackle them, like extra power inside me. And I had help from the other Christians at church, especially in the women's Bible study group. I began telling others about how God had changed my life. I saw that I was less selfish. My marriage improved and my relationship with my children improved, mostly, I think, because I was improved myself. There was this deep sense of calm in my heart, or head, or wherever you have that kind of feeling. I became a changed person. This first excitement and joy continued for more than a year. It was wonderful! Two of my coworkers started coming to church with me off and on, and my husband even started coming once a month or so. One of my friends at work eventually became a Christian too, and we started a little Bible study once a week during lunch at the office.

> "I don't mean to suggest I was perfect. In fact, I still did wrong things sometimes. But I had a totally new desire inside to please Christ. I had power to live right. My life was completely changed when I became a Christian."

"I don't mean to suggest I was perfect. In fact, I still did wrong things sometimes. But I had a totally new desire inside to please Christ. I had power to live right. My life was completely changed when I became a Christian. I became a different person and it seems to me I was doing everything God could ever expect from me."

GRADUAL GROWTH

"Then I discovered a new problem. As I read the Bible, attended Sunday school and our women's Bible study, I began realizing that

God's expectations were pretty high. In fact they seemed higher than I could reach. I saw that he wanted total obedience to the Bible. I learned the Bible called me to be Christlike, to be transformed even more than I already was. This seemed completely impossible to me, yet I kept sensing this was what God wanted. At conversion I had received a new desire to obey Christ. I was no longer a slave of Satan. But, along with this desire to obey, I still had a desire to serve myself at times. In fact, it seemed there was a constant tug-of-war inside me—the Holy Spirit was on one end, my old desires were on the other, and I was the rope!

"Usually, I sided with my new life in Christ and obeyed God. But sometimes I sided with my old life and disobeyed the Lord. At first these incidents of disobedience did not seem so bad—after all, compared to what I was before, I was still better off. But as time passed, I began feeling convicted about even the 'little' incidents of sin. After each time of failure I would feel terrible. I knew that the Bible called me to obey, yet often I just wasn't able to pull it off. Some of the 'new convert glow' was wearing off. I noticed that I was less intent on sharing Jesus with others, and sometimes I was depressed about my own failures and inability to change more.

"But I continued to grow as a Christian. God would make new demands on my life—to stop some bad habit or to start a good habit. I often struggled a long time over these issues. I wanted to please Christ, but I also wanted to keep some of the practices, thoughts, and habits from my old life. In a way I was still traveling on two tracks. Even when I knew God wanted me to change, I often resisted him. These two competing desires plagued me: a desire to live for God and a desire to live for myself. I sometimes got so weary from the struggle that I wanted to give up. The first year after I was saved was wonderful. The second year was awful!

"Each time God brought 'new light' to me about something I needed to stop or start, I generally responded in three stages."

Stage One—Denial. "I remember when he convicted me of a certain habit I had carried over from my old life. I guess I can tell you what is was. I was reading some pretty salacious romance novels. I would buy sacks full of them at a used bookstore in our town and gulp them down like chocolate. It was a habit for me.

"I never even thought they were that bad until I attended a marriage seminar at our church where the speakers talked to the men about pornography. As the couple holding the seminar was describing the difference between men's and women's temptations, they just mentioned romance novels in passing, calling them 'women's pornography.' I was startled. I refused to equate my innocent romance novels with the terrible porn that men sometimes look at.

"But God began to talk to me about it. Nobody at church said anything, but I knew God was talking. My first response was to deny it. I rationalized my reading habit as normal, human, even helpful. I told myself, *I'm not perfect—just forgiven.* Why should I stop? So, for a while, I simply denied my need and ignored God's conviction. If you refuse to confess, you don't have to change, I figured.

"However, the Holy Spirit kept knocking. The more I ignored him, the more persistent he got. Finally, I realized that if I continued reading this stuff I'd be flat out disobeying God. I saw that my refusal to listen to God was affecting my relationship with him. Finally I admitted my novels chained me up and pulled me away from my husband (and God). I admitted that God wanted to change me. I remember the women's Bible study that morning. We divided into 'prayer triplets' at the end of the meeting. Each of us was to share how God had been dealing with us recently. I heard myself blurting out, 'God's been bugging me about reading romance novels, and I've been ignoring him. Please pray that I'll have strength to stop.' The two other women prayed especially for me that day. I had quit denying God's conviction. I had confessed."

Stage Two—Delay. "But I didn't get victory that quickly. I merely entered a second stage. True, I had admitted I should stop reading those novels. But now, I tried to delay obedience as long as possible. 'I've got to finish this book and find out how it ends, Lord.' Then after that I said, 'Just one more book, then I'll quit.' And even after that I said, 'I'll quit after I've read the books I've already purchased.' I was convinced I needed to kill off this habit. I was convinced that God wanted it to end. But I had not yet decided to obey. I was delaying obedience. A long struggle ensued.

I'd promise myself I'd quit, but I'd break the promise before long. I kept saying, 'Eventually I am going to stop.' But inside I was emphasizing the 'eventually' part!

"The Holy Spirit didn't give up on me. He kept convicting me. But now, he had a powerful ally— my mind where I had already admitted my need. My mind was

> "At conversion I had received a new desire to obey Christ. I was no longer a slave of Satan. But, along with this desire to obey, I still had a desire to serve myself at times. In fact, it seemed there was a constant tug-of-war inside me— the Holy Spirit was on one end, my old desires were on the other, and I was the rope!"

made up even though my life lagged behind my mind. The Spirit and my mind worked together on my will. Of course, the Devil encouraged me to keep delaying. The tension inside me during this second stage was sometimes unbearable. I knew obedience was the right choice, yet I still wanted to continue my habit just a little longer. I felt like such a rotten Christian. I wished I could go back and be like I was my first year as a Christian—I read these books then without any conviction!

"On this particular issue of reading romance novels, an interesting event brought about my surrender. Our younger son takes out the garbage each day when he returns from school. I often have to remind him once or twice of this chore. On one particular day, he was especially slow to respond. I had reminded him four or five times before we sat down to supper. After supper I noticed the garbage was still not carried out. I was exasperated and I shouted, 'This is the last time I am going to remind you. Take out the garbage . . . NOW!' He left the table and I figured he had done his chore.

> "I continued to grow as a Christian. God would make new demands on my life—to stop some bad habit or to start a good habit. I often struggled a long time over these issues. I wanted to please Christ, but I also wanted to keep some of the practices, thoughts, and habits from my old life."

"I later discovered the garbage was still piled in the kitchen— he had gotten sidetracked again. We had a 'serious talk' that night. I explained to my son how continued delay in obedience eventually becomes outright disobedience. His foot-dragging had, in fact, become disobedience."

Stage Three—Obedience. "Then it hit me like a ton of bricks. That was exactly what I had been doing with God! I knew what he wanted and even said I'd obey him. Yet I had delayed obeying what I knew he was telling me. I was delaying, just like my son! I went to the bedroom and knelt down by the bed. I took the third step— full obedience. That afternoon I surrendered to him my reading habits and asked for deliverance. I took the remainder of my books out to the garbage can myself that night.

"I had gone through three stages: denial, delay, and then finally obedience. In fact, these three stages pretty well describe a lot of my growth during the following years as a Christian. First, I would deny my need and ignore that 'still small voice.' Then when I admitted God was right, I'd delay obeying for a while, and finally, I'd surrender that area and come into full obedience.

"Then God would let me go for a while and eventually he would nudge me in a new area to change. After another period of conviction and struggle I would eventually come to full obedience in this new area and so on. Each time I surrendered and obeyed I'd be full of joy for a while. Then he'd begin tapping on a new area of change I needed to make."

THE BIGGER PROBLEM—ME

"But this is not the whole story. It wouldn't be honest to say that I eventually obeyed in all the areas where the Lord convicted. Actually, there were two or three areas where I continued to resist Christ's Lordship. I guess I simply posted a 'no trespassing' sign before these thoughts, habits, and attitudes. I decided to reserve them for myself. This was a new realization to me: the essential problem in this struggle was not this or that thing God was speaking about. It was me. It was my self-will. I kept denying the need or delaying change. Why? Because I wanted to be in charge myself. These competing desires in my heart troubled me. I sometimes felt like the battlefield between good and evil ran right through my own heart—and I was on both sides of the battle at once!

"I wished there was a way to be free of this inclination inside me to always have my own way. I wished for a way to be totally and wholly committed to God and his work in me. I was tired of resisting him before yielding. I was growing, but painfully."

> "I knew what he wanted and even said I'd obey him. Yet I had delayed obeying what I knew he was telling me. I went to the bedroom and knelt down by the bed. I took the third step—full obedience."

A NEW HOPE

"Then I heard about being filled completely by the Holy Spirit and 'entire sanctification.' I had heard this idea before, but this time the truth really came home. I heard that God wanted to be in total command of my life. He wanted to replace my divided desire with a heart full of love for him and others. They told me that God wanted to fill me with power to serve him. He wanted to make my heart pure. Undivided. Cleansed. It sounded too good to be true. But I saw my situation clearly. Satan's ally inside me was me. My own self-will repeatedly struggled against God's will for me. The more I studied the Bible in our women's group, the more I saw God's call to complete obedience to him and love for others. I knew that I fell far short of what he expected. More than that, I knew that I honestly didn't even fully want to be totally Christlike. My desire was divided. I wanted to be holy, but I also wanted to be self-centered at the same time.

"I began to realize that God was not only convicting me about the few areas I had been holding out, but He was making claims on something bigger—my will itself. He wanted me to settle the matter of how serious I was about obeying him—completely obeying his will. At this point it was no longer about 'little things' like surrendering romance novels or my language or the movies I watched. It was no longer about starting to tithe or getting involved in teaching Sunday school. Now God wanted me to surrender me. He wanted me to totally surrender to him as the master of my life. He wanted me to give him everything. Make him master and Lord. He was asking me to settle the matter once and for all, who would be 'boss' in my life. A magazine article I read promised that if I really made a 'living sacrifice'—a dedication of myself to God—he would cleanse me of this rebellious nature. I doubted the whole idea for a long time. I wanted it to be true, but I kept saying, 'If it looks too good to be true, it probably isn't true.'

"It just didn't seem possible that God could make my desires pure and wholly obedient to him. My inclination to selfishness and disobedience had so long been a part of me. I was, however, hopeful enough to read about it. I began reading books. I started talking with several other older Christians about it. Our women's Bible study even began a series on holiness and I thought there was a conspiracy against me! I still had doubts about the idea, but at the same time I got hungrier the more I read and talked to people. I started seeing this idea in the Bible. Almost all the Christians I respected seemed to have had some sort of moment when they 'sold out completely' to Christ and God changed them. I eventually came to believe that God might just be willing to do this for me."

MY CONSECRATION

"I still did not make a total surrender to Christ for a while. I believed I eventually would—yet I delayed. Then I realized I was going through the very same stages I so often had followed in the individual areas of growth before. In each case where I had obeyed, I could now see how it was for my own good. God wasn't trying to make me miserable; he wanted to make my life full and complete. I was doing laundry one day when this realization dawned on me. God wanted all of me because he knows best. He wanted what is best for me. I sat down on my bed and cried, 'I'm yours, Lord—I want you to be the boss of my life. I will no longer delay—from this day forward you have all of me. Everything.' My will surrendered to Christ. I didn't just say the words—I meant it. I surrendered all to Jesus. It was finished. I sighed with a great sense of relief.

"Something happened that day. Something I didn't understand at first. God responded and it was like getting saved all over again. Now I know: God cleansed my heart that day. My inclination to disobey melted. I was full of love for God like I never knew before.

God purified my divided heart. He filled me with his Holy Spirit, or baptized me with the Holy Spirit, or I entered into an Upper Room Experience, or whatever you want to call it. I didn't even understand the terms then but something happened that was profound."

YEARS LATER

"Looking back, I now realize that God had been gradually preparing me for that moment of total surrender to him. Following the big changes at my conversion, he had progressively drawn me closer to him. All this was in preparation for a new relationship and walk of total obedience and love. In fact, the gradual process of conviction, surrender, and victory was a template of sorts for the complete work of sanctification which came later.

"I have several friends today who are, right now, in this period of gradual growth, or progressive sanctification. They're winning the battle part of the time. Yet, at other times they are painfully aware that their inner selfish desires are often contrary to God's will. We started meeting together before work on Tuesdays for accountability. I can see how God is working in their lives. He is bringing both of my friends to the place where they are getting new hope. They are hoping they can be cleansed of the divided heart, but they are afraid it cannot happen. But their hope is growing. They are hungry that they will someday be able to completely follow Christ because they are so full of love for him. They want to be totally transformed into obedient and submissive servants of Christ and others. I can see that God is leading them down a road

> "The essential problem in this struggle was not this or that thing God was speaking about. It was me. It was my self-will. I kept denying the need or delaying change. Why? Because I wanted to be in charge myself."

similar to the one I took. It won't be long now until their hunger will lead to filling."

Of course, every individual is different, and your own growth in progressive sanctification may tell a different story. However, Sue's example illustrates how a believer is transformed at conversion and grows in grace as we approach the call to entire sanctification. Here's the point of this chapter: if we continually obey the Lord, we will progressively draw closer to Christ until our walk leads us to a moment when we face the question of total surrender to God. It's not that we chose one or the other kind of sanctification—progressive or entire, progressive sanctification leads to entire sanctification and the life thereafter.

GOD'S PART IN SANCTIFICATION **8**

When we study God's work in men and women, we should always look at both sides of the coin—God's part and our part. God seldom works in us without our participation and cooperation. God does his part. We do our part. This chapter focuses on what God does when we're filled with the Holy Spirit or entirely sanctified. The next chapter will focus on our part— what *we* do in cooperating with God's part.

So, what does God actually do when he entirely sanctifies us by his Holy Spirit? What changes should occur in our daily lives?

How will we be different? The changes accomplished in us through entire sanctification may be organized into two general categories: (1) power over sin—correction of our inward inclination to disobey God, and (2) power for loving service—renewed energy for serving God and others.

Of course, most denominations have a doctrine of sanctification. We have to. It's in the Bible. Check it out. Just about all denominations provide for some sort of after-conversion consecration to the Lord that results in greater power and love.

However, like all truths with two aspects, denominations tend to emphasize one aspect or the other: either power over sin, or power for loving service. For instance some have emphasized the power over sin side so much that they almost ignore the power for loving service side. These Christians talk a lot about victory over sin and living in obedience. They talk about deliverance from lust, covetousness, pride, complacency, envy, impure thoughts, selfish ambition, rage, jealousy, self-will, and other sins of the flesh and spirit. People on this end of the spectrum tend toward separation from the world. In fact, they ultimately may come to test their experience by how much they resist "worldliness." The proof of complete sanctification to them is often defined by what they don't do. Admittedly, people in the traditional Holiness movement have been liable to this overemphasis—looking mostly at the power-over-sin side of this work.

But the other side of the coin can be overemphasized too. People on this side emphasize power for loving service and ignore the sin question almost entirely. They are inclined to cite powerful attitudes of love or energetic soul-winning or service to the world as the best evidence of the Spirit's baptism. To them, sanctification is for service. No service, no sanctification. While the first group tends to diminish the importance of loving service, this second group diminishes the seriousness of sin.

Face it; our own personal experience affects how we perceive doctrine. For instance, two individuals who have experienced entire sanctification may strongly disagree on which aspect is predominant.

Take Jerry, for instance. He had been very active in church work for years. He taught a Sunday school class, served as a trustee, sang in the choir, and was one of the most faithful members to show up for the visiting program on Tuesday nights. Yet he struggled with a secret sin nobody knew about. He tried to beat it, but had little victory. Finally, Jerry made a total consecration to the Lord and sought deliverance from this inner sin. He was desperate. And God did respond, though not right away. When Jerry experienced complete victory, God did more than he had asked for. While Jerry had only sought deliverance from one particular sinful drive, God responded with a total cleansing in his life. Jerry found victory over other sinful areas in his life, indeed all other areas of willful sin. His inner nature was cleansed. He saw tremendous differences in his life. His new inner purity enabled him to get constant victory over that stubborn sin—in fact, victory over all purposeful sin.

> God seldom works in us without our participation and cooperation. God does his part. We do our part.

Jerry was able to honestly tell his two accountability partners that he had "lived all last month in total obedience to everything God was commanding me to do." A month of total obedience! After struggling all those years, Jerry felt as free as a bird. The heavy weight was gone. He felt clean. He had been delivered from a body of death hanging around his neck. He later came to understand the totality of the work God had done for him.

Now, how will Jerry talk about the results of being entirely sanctified? How will he teach a class on this subject? What will he emphasize? Power for loving service? Probably not. He had been serving in the Lord's work for years, and he saw only minor changes in his loving service. What will he emphasize? Power over sin. He will talk about how God purified his heart. He'll testify to new power over sin. He may totally ignore the power-for-service side of the work.

However, Jerry's wife Marilyn has another story. Marilyn never had big trouble with sin. At least she didn't feel that way. Ever since she became a Christian she had been a "good Christian." In fact Marilyn seemed to be a better Christian before she became a Christian than many Christians are afterward. Her problem was not a sin of thought or word. Her trouble was not action, but inaction. Marilyn's sin problem didn't look like sin on the surface: it was being lukewarm, passive, and uninvolved. She simply coasted along in her Christian life and seldom showed passion.

> "I knew what he wanted and even said I'd obey him. Yet I had delayed obeying what I knew he was telling me. I went to the bedroom and knelt down by the bed. I took the third step—full obedience."

She knew people without Christ were lost, but she didn't feel any burden for them. She knew the church needed Sunday school teachers and VBS workers, but she never volunteered. She was a Christian, and as far as doing any sinful act, she seemed perfect. Marilyn's sin problem was not in what she did, but in what she did not do.

Finally Marilyn became dissatisfied with her passionless relationship with God. At a retreat she totally dedicated her life to God. She "died out" to her coolness and "life of triviality." She wanted power from God to make a difference in her world. God responded with new power. What did she notice? Power over sin? Not really, at least not sin in the action sense. What she saw was a power for loving service. She experienced a new burst of spiritual energy for God's work. She felt a burden for her lost neighbors for the first time in her life. She had been saying, "It just doesn't fit my personality," when they tried to recruit her for the calling program. Now she became burdened enough for lost souls to overcome her natural reluctance. She signed up. What happened to Marilyn? She was entirely sanctified. But she experienced the power-for-service aspect of the work more clearly in her life. So, how will she describe this experience? It will probably be mostly about power for service, not power over sin.

Both power over sin and power for loving service are two sides of the same experience. When God does his work of entire sanctification, it results in a definite victory over willful sin—even inward sin. But we also experience a new power for loving service in order to do God's work in the world—winning others to Christ, helping believers grow, and establishing the kingdom of Christ on earth. We may personally experience one aspect more dramatically than another. Our denomination may emphasize one aspect more than the other, but it's not an either/or proposition. Both aspects of power result from this work of God.

POWER OVER SIN

What kind of sin-power can I expect? Does God deliver me from all sin forever? Will I be absolutely perfect from that moment onward? Is this instant Christlikeness? Microwave perfection? Sinless perfection?

There is more confusion and misunderstanding over this one point than any other holiness teaching. Some argue that holiness people teach an instant perfection: a believer becomes completely perfect—exactly like Jesus Christ—at entire sanctification. They say holiness teaching calls for a perfect life where there is no need for any further growth—ever. I doubt that this view has ever actually been taught much, but people believe it was taught, so the error needs to be addressed. The notion is simply false.

The root cause of this misunderstanding is confusion over the statement, "It's possible to be delivered from all sin." Anyone who makes such a statement (and I would make it) had better know what he means by "sin."

There are two general ideas of sin. Both are in the Bible, in both the Old and New Testaments. If you understand these two general ideas of sin, it resolves many theological and doctrinal arguments. Here are the two ideas of sin.

TWO UNDERSTANDINGS OF SIN

Idea 1: Sin Is Purposeful Disobedience. This idea says sin is knowing something is wrong and doing it anyway—on purpose. Sin is knowing God's will and refusing to obey. This kind of sin is premeditated, purposeful, and intentional. This idea sees sin as willful disobedience of God.

Idea 2: Sin Is Falling Short of Christlikeness. This idea of sin (also in the Bible) focuses on God's standard of perfect holiness. God's standard is Jesus Christ's perfection. Anything that falls short of that is sin. Any word, thought, or deed that is less than perfect Christlikeness is sin. Any unsaid word, unthought thought, undone deed that falls short of what Christ would say, think, or do is sin. Falling short. The thought, word, or deed could be accidental or done without premeditation or even knowing that the thing is wrong. It does not matter. The standard is fixed, and any deviation from the perfect standard is sin. This second idea of sin includes both purposeful transgressions, plus the thousands of accidental or innocent times we fall short of God's perfection.

Can you see how these two ideas of sin affect a Christian's theology? For instance, a person with the second idea of sin (falling short) can easily say, "I sin every day in word, thought, and deed." Of course we all fall short of God's absolute perfection every day.

That person would be right (given the second definition of sin). All of us sin every day, if we mean sin is everything that falls short of perfection.

When we say in this book that God can enable us to "live above sin," we mean the first idea of sin (purposeful, knowing disobedience) not the second idea. Living above sin here means living without purposefully rebelling against or defying God. Entire sanctification can enable us to live without purposefully rebelling against what we know God wants. It's the power to stop willfully sinning against the

> When God does his work of entire sanctification, it results in a definite victory over willful sin—even inward sin. But we also experience a new power for loving service in order to do God's work in the world—winning others to Christ, helping believers grow, and establishing the kingdom of Christ on earth.

Lord. It's the power to obey. It's not the power to be absolutely perfect in the sense of absolute Christlikeness. We still will fall short of his perfect standard (idea 2).

John Wesley called the first idea of sin (purposeful disobedience), *sin, strictly speaking* (as opposed to the second idea: *sin, generally speaking*). Though we still might fall short of God's perfect standard, we can be considered blameless if our will is in total submission to the Lord and we are obeying all the light or leading we have received. Of course, this blamelessness cannot be used as an excuse for laziness about growth. As God reveals areas where we fall short and prompts us to change, we become responsible for this light.

This idea should not be strange to anyone who is a parent. If a thirteen-month-old child knocks over her milk because of her immature clumsiness, will she get disciplined? No. She clearly falls far short of the perfect standard of table manners. But no sensible parent would punish this child. The parent overlooks this behavior because of the child's stage of development. The child is "blameless."

However, suppose you have an eight-year-old son. And he is fooling around at the dinner table, and you've tried to correct him. You gave him several warnings to straighten up, but he keeps giggling and kicking his brother under the table. You warn, "Watch out, or you'll spill your milk." Then he looks up into your eyes, and a brazen look comes over his face. He deliberately reaches out his forefinger and knocks over his glass of milk gazing defiantly into your face. Milk splatters everywhere and begins dripping onto your dining room carpet. How will you react to this deliberate rebellion? He'd better run! This second kind of behavior is what we call *sin, strictly speaking*. This is the kind of sin every Christian can be free of.

The power-over-sin aspect of entire sanctification will not prevent us from falling short of God's perfect standard. However, God is able to purify our hearts so that we will not willfully disobey him when we clearly know what he wants. This is the power over sin that God promises in entire sanctification.

Some argue that holiness people teach an instant perfection: a believer becomes completely perfect—exactly like Jesus Christ—at entire sanctification. I doubt that this view has ever actually been taught much, but people believe it was taught, so the error needs to be addressed. The notion is simply false.

After following the Lord for awhile, most Christians recognize an inclination to disobey God is still present inside. This inclination can lead us into repeated disobedience and failure. The work of the Holy Spirit in entire sanctification deals with this inclination—the nature toward sin. God can cleanse, purify, and correct our driven-ness to disobey—so that we're able to walk in habitual obedience to all the Lord commands. Because of our immaturity, inadequacies, and humanness, we will still fall short of Christ's perfect standard of righteousness. But if our will is totally submitted to him, God can overlook our immature spilt milk. Wouldn't you, as an earthly parent, do as much? God will do even better. God is the perfect parent.

So, when we emphasize the power-over-sin side of entire sanctification, we mean that God is able to cleanse us from the inclination to disobey him so that it's possible to live without purposeful, defiant sin.

POWER FOR SERVICE

What is God's work in the world? It's to save lost sinners, help believers become more like Christ, and establish the kingdom of God world-wide. What is the greatest hindrance to God's work? Us. God has no other hands, but ours. He has chosen to use his children to accomplish his work of evangelism, discipleship, establishing justice, and caring for the hurting.

Why do so many Christians do so little to accomplish God's work? Why do so few actually evangelize the lost, disciple other Christians toward maturity, feed the hungry, aid the poor, and establish justice? Why do 20 percent of the people do 80 percent of the work around the church? Because there are so many Christians who have never been filled completely with the love of God. They have never received the power of love (or have lost the blessing after receiving it).

Why then does God want us to surrender and receive his empowering work? So he can use us to accomplish his work in the world—evangelizing the lost, leading believers to maturity, and establishing the kingdom of God. What is the kingdom of God? It is a world where his will is done on earth as it is in heaven. Spirit-filled believers do not sit on the sidelines of life waiting for the ejection button to be pushed so they can go to heaven. We "work 'til Jesus comes," establishing the sort of world that is based on kingdom values.

Sanctification is for service. Service means being sent. Sent where? Sent to other Christians and sent to a world God loves and Christ died for. When Jesus prayed for his disciples' sanctification in John 17, he spoke of their being sent into the world—not that they should be taken out of it. Sanctification means being sent.

The power of the Holy Spirit is not just to deal with sin. It is to ignite a life of loving service. It provides power to work in the dirty trenches of daily life, yet remain unspotted. There is power to take the light of the gospel to dark corners. There is power to carry our salty preventative presence into a rotting deteriorating world. It provides power to work with lepers, those with AIDS, to care for the poor, to provide hope to the hopeless, food for the hungry, clothing for the naked, companionship for the lonely. This is the witness so desperately needed today. The world is tired of Christians who build walls and toss grenades over the wall at sinners telling them how bad they are. The world is hungry for Christians who tear down their judgmental walls and enter the world showing them what the unbelievers know in their heart that a Christian should be like. This is the powerful witness that comes by loving service to the needy. After the Holy Spirit comes upon us, we *shall* be witnesses. There is both power over sin and power for service in sanctification.

CONCLUSION

Most believers sooner or later recognize one or both of these problems: (1) there is sin they can't beat; or (2) there is power they don't have. The root cause of both of these problems is self-will. The reason we're disobedient is because we decide to disobey. The cause of our complacency is our decision to remain complacent. If God is not the master of our life, the reason is we have decided to be our own boss. Here is the essential issue of total consecration: the decision about who will be the "boss." If we're willing to make God the Lord of our lives and reach out in faith to trust him to perform a new work in us, we can receive God's full and perfect love inside us. His love will produce: (1) power over sin, for if we love him we will keep his commandments; and (2) power for loving service, because if we love our neighbor as ourselves, we can do nothing but plunge into the world in loving service.

> Entire sanctification can enable us to live without purposefully rebelling against what we know God wants. It's the power to stop willfully sinning against the Lord. It's the power to obey.

If you are totally satisfied with your level of victory over sin and you think your life is already filled with loving service to others, then this truth will fly right over your head (or perhaps you have already experienced what this book is talking about). But if you are discouraged about some sin you can't beat or spiritual power you don't have, then seek the Holy Spirit's complete filling with love in entire sanctification. The one who calls you is faithful and he will do it.

OUR PART IN SANCTIFICATION 9

There are two parts to sanctification: God's part and our part. God's part is purifying and energizing. Our part is consecration and faith.

Down through history, believers who wrote, spoke, and testified to this deeper walk with God have variously placed greater emphasis on either God's part or our part. This is still true today. Some talk with great enthusiasm about God's part. They may give the impression that God does this work in whomever he pleases, whenever he wants to, and perhaps for reasons unknown to the recipient. To them, there is little we can do to receive entire sanctification except wait until God sanctifies us fully. These Christians give little emphasis to consecration or "taking it by faith." They argue that God alone has his own mysterious timetable for making us holy, and he will do so when he is good and ready. There is little urgency to seek entire sanctification since we would be trespassing on God's territory—only God knows when he plans to give this gift—grabbing it is impolite. This describes the thinking of those who emphasize God's part alone.

However, there are others who downplay God's part in sanctification and upgrade our part—consecration and faith. Taking a most logical approach, they say: (1) consecrate your total life to God; (2) having done that, realize the Bible says God will cleanse you and fill you with spiritual power; (3) so, simply believe that God has done

> It's our responsibility to consecrate our "all to Jesus." He will not do this for us. He will not blast down the door of our life and rip our life from our own hands. God has limited the boundaries of his work by the free will of men and women. He has granted you and me the right to refuse.

what he promised. Consider yourself cleansed. That's that! It's over. Take it by faith—like you became a Christian in the first place.

This book teaches both of these extremes are out of balance. But both sides help us see the total picture. There are two parts to sanctification: God's part and our part. God alone works in us to sanctify us, but he does so with our cooperation. Sanctification is not just a unilateral activity of God but bilateral—both God and us are involved in this act. We are changed through a partnership with God. He has his part in doing the work, and we have ours in coming to him in consecration and faith.

But be sure to know that even though we have a part, God alone does the cleansing and empowerment. We cannot do it ourselves. How many times have we said to wrong attitudes, thoughts, and affections, "Be gone!" yet they remain? How often have we tried to work up spiritual energy to witness or to minister to others, yet we fail to have true spiritual power? We cannot cleanse our own bent to sinning. We cannot energize ourselves. This is God's work and God's alone. Only he can cleanse our heart from its disposition to disobey. Only he can energize our life for ministry to a hurting world. It takes his grace and his power. This is his work alone.

However, we have a part to play. It's our responsibility to consecrate our "all to Jesus." He will not do this for us. He will not blast down the door of our life and rip our life from our own hands. God has limited the boundaries of his work by the free will of men and women. He has granted you and me the right to refuse.

God wants us to dedicate our whole life to him. All of us. He yearns for our total trust in him. He longs for our faith in him to cleanse and energize us. Yet it will not happen until we consecrate our life to him and believe he will cleanse us. True, in a sense, even this act of consecration can be credited to him—he convicts us and tenderly brings us to a place of decision. So we can take no credit for sanctifying ourselves and we can't even take all the credit for a total consecration. God is even the author of our faith, since the earliest conviction comes from him. Yet, we're most likely the ones who hold up the process of sanctification, not God. It's our stubbornness. Our resistance. Our foot-dragging. Our sin that holds up God's complete sanctification in our heart. Until we break down and seek him, he does not complete his work.

Sanctification is accomplished through a partnership with God. We consecrate and believe; God cleanses and energizes. With our consecration and faith, he purifies and empowers. In the preceding chapter, we examined *God's part* in entire sanctification—purifying and energizing. In this chapter, we will examine *our part*—consecration and faith.

OUR PART: CONSECRATION

John's testimony describes what consecration is:

"After I had walked with God for several years, two things gradually became painfully apparent to me: (1) there was power available from God which I did not have; and (2) I was naturally inclined to disobey the Lord and fought an inner battle between two desires. This realization came to me gradually, but it grew in strength over the months and years after my conversion. Eventually I became convinced that I wasn't where I ought to be—there must be something more.

"I had heard about total consecration and entire sanctification dozens of times. I had always shrugged it off as something too hard to understand. But last winter it all began to sink in. It was as if a seed of truth had quietly found a hiding place in a crevice of my mind. It began to sprout into a tiny bit of faith. I started believing that maybe I could be delivered from my inner resistance to God. I began to hope that there *was* more spiritual power available than I had. I started reading about the subject, and I asked a few friends. Most of them didn't understand sanctification either, so they offered little help.

"Then I got to know Tom. I had always admired his dedicated work in the church. And I knew how he regularly shared his faith with others and was always caring for people in need. He was a powerful, yet tender man. He invited me to meet each Tuesday at 6:30 A.M. for a Bible study and personal accountability. As we studied and shared together, he unfolded the truth about sanctification over the next few months in such a clear way. I knew I needed this work even though I wasn't completely sure it was possible. It seemed possible for him—but not for me. Tom told how God had done a special work in his life several years back—even before he even heard about entire sanctification. I came gradually to believe that it might happen to me too. Tom helped me pray. I finally came to the place where I totally committed my life to Christ—all of me. I understood what that meant. It took a while to 'die out' but I eventually surrendered all to Jesus.

"My real struggle surrounded one particular area which I had never allowed the Lord to control. On the Tuesday that God sanctified me, I was carefully committing my total life to him again (for the tenth time) when this one area popped up in my mind. I quickly passed over it and began listing other things I had already committed to God. But the Holy Spirit kept bringing my mind back to that one area. I guess it was my real area of holdout.

> Entire consecration is an act of giving Christ control of our total life. It's a one-time dedication of our all to Jesus, holding nothing back. It's unreserved surrender. It's a covenant with the Lord to always obey his prompting. It's a vow to submit to his will for our life and walk in obedience, not trusting our own energy, but his. It's surrender.

"Finally, Tom helped me understand my resistance in this area for what it really was—rebellion against Christ's lordship. I felt crushed. Here I was *almost* totally surrendered to God, yet not 100 percent consecrated. Tom gently reminded me of the parallel in marriage. He asked how I would have responded if my wife had told me at our wedding that she would forsake all other men on earth, except one, to marry me. Would I have been satisfied? Until he made the marriage connection, I had figured I was a pretty committed guy. After all, I had given up almost everything to God. But seeing it through the eyes of a husband changed everything. My holdout in this one area seemed so much worse now. I was not committed any more than a bride who reserved the right to romance one other man besides her husband.

"I broke. That morning I surrendered to Christ this personal area I'd clung to for so long. I trusted by faith that he had cleansed me and filled me.

"Nothing happened! I didn't feel any different. Tom instructed me to keep seeking until I found what God had for me. I left that breakfast meeting assuming I was unchanged. But I was wrong. I started to see the difference the next day. Within two weeks my life had taken on a totally different character. I was hesitant at first to say anything about it. It was like walking on eggs. I didn't want to do anything to ruin this new joy, power, and peace I had experienced.

"I wondered why I had held out so long. After all, I knew who Jesus was and all he had done for me. Why didn't I trust him with everything sooner? Why did I think I could do better at managing my life than he could? I don't know. But within a month, I knew that God had done a second, major work in my life. It was dramatic. I had new power over sin. I had energy for service and love for people I never had loved before. My usual selfishness was crippled. There was a deep peace in my soul. I was hungry for the things of God. My life has been wonderfully different ever since."

> In total consecration, we decide to make Jesus the permanent master of all of our life. We become permanent slaves—love slaves. In total consecration, we place everything in his hands—our burdens, our striving, our pains and hurts, our weaknesses, and even our faults. This is the complete consecration that opens up our heart for complete sanctification. God will sanctify whatever we put in his hands.

John's testimony illustrates consecration. God urges us to give all to him. He wants us to make a total surrender of our lives to him. The emphasis is on *total*. He wants all of us—our time, our talents, our thoughts, our finances, our hopes, our aspirations, our reputation, our hobbies, our friendships, our habits, and our future. He wants to be the Lord and master of every part of our lives. He knows what is best for us. He tenderly urges us to turn over to him our all. He wants to use us and direct, guide, and change us into the image of his perfect Son. With our cooperation and consecration, he will cleanse and empower. His response in power and cleansing is not always right away. For some there is a long wait even after a total consecration but for most of us what holds us up is lack of full consecration.

The cleansing is available—available for *you*. The power is ready—ready for you. Why don't you have it? Is it because God is withholding it? Probably not. It's more likely because you have not totally and completely given yourself over to God—in complete consecration. This is your part. Consecration.

Any of us who have walked with God for a time recognize that God regularly urges us to consecrate to him one area or another. This *progressive consecration* opens us up to the *progressive sanctification* we spoke of earlier. It gets us ready for entire consecration and entire sanctification. Can you think of several areas you've gradually turned over to the Lord? What did He do? You remember. He moved into that part of your life with power. He rearranged and changed things. But now, God is not asking for this or that area of consecration. He asks for everything. For all. One hundred percent. This is *entire consecration*, which opens us up to receive God's *entire sanctification*. God will cleanse what he gets from you even if there is a lag between your entire consecration and his response with entire sanctification. If you give him part, he'll sanctify part. If you give him all, he'll sanctify all.

Entire consecration is the act of giving Christ control of our total life. It's a one-time dedication of our all to Jesus, holding nothing back. It's unreserved surrender. It's a covenant with the Lord to always obey his prompting. It's a vow to submit to his will for our life and walk in obedience, not trusting our own energy, but his. It's surrender.

Jesus is our example. What did he pray in the garden? "Not my will, but Yours be done." This is the prayer of entire consecration: total surrender to God's will and way. It's holding nothing back. It's saying, "From this day forward, I am yours, Lord. I will walk in total obedience to Your will, not mine." In total consecration, we decide to make Jesus the permanent master of all of our life. We become permanent slaves—love slaves. In total consecration, we place everything in his hands—our burdens, our striving, our pains and hurts, our weaknesses, and even our faults. We live a life of trust, not trying, but trusting. Our total reliance from then on will be on Jesus alone. He will be my consuming passion for living—the absorbing desire of my heart, my cause for living. This is the complete consecration that opens up our heart for complete sanctification. God will sanctify whatever we put in his hands.

But understand that all this is more than feeling. Entire consecration is an act of the will. We are, with firm intentions, placing our "all on the altar," as a sacrifice to God. We want him—only him—to rule our thoughts, our habits, our words, and our deeds from now through eternity. We're making an entire surrender, a total abandonment to God—spirit, soul, and body placed under his absolute management. We're making a clear-minded determination to obey Christ, whatever the cost—a vow to a life of obedience. This is total consecration.

Does this idea appeal to you? Then why not do it now? God does not want your total commitment in order to make you miserable. He wants to give you the greatest joy and fulfillment imaginable! Are you totally consecrated to God, holding nothing back? Why not trust him now? You can trust him. Doesn't all this talk of total surrender to Jesus make sense? Do you hunger for this kind of walk with God? Is God gently calling you to this? Do you hunger for this? *Now*? Why not lay down this book right now and go to prayer?

OUR PART: FAITH

Entire consecration is the first half of our part in receiving God's sanctification. Faith is the second part. Both consecration and faith are our assignments. Without faith there is no entire sanctification. We must believe God, believe that God will do what he promised, and believe he will do it now. This is faith. He still may tarry, but more often he responds immediately.

Faith is not feeling. It's not some sort of bubbly, inner excitement that gives us an enthusiastic anticipation that God is going to perform a miracle in our lives.

Neither is faith desire. We may hunger and thirst to be cleansed and energized. We may desire it more than we want popularity, power, wealth, food, drink—even our next breath. Desire is vital, but desire alone is not faith.

Faith isn't hope either. We may someday hope to be entirely sanctified. We could say, "He might do it—he could do it—it's possible." But this is not enough. This is hope, not faith.

> Without faith there is no entire sanctification. We must believe God, believe that God will do what he promised, and believe he will do it now. This is faith. He still may tarry, but more often he responds immediately.

And faith is not mental assent. We may accept the fact that God cleanses and energizes following our consecration. We may see this truth in God's Word and believe it. We can accept it as true, recite it as our creed, and even teach it as dogma. But accepting the truth is not faith.

All of these factors have a part in our receiving entire sanctification. Feeling, desire, hope, and belief are all a basis of sanctification. But none of these are sanctifying faith. We receive God's provisions for us when we reach out in faith and receive them. Sanctifying faith is trusting in Christ's promise now. It's receiving now. It's receiving cleansing and power by faith, now. It's more than saying, "I want this work." It's saying, "I receive this work in my heart—right here and right now." The one who calls us is faithful, and he will do it. Faith believes he has done it.

Even love includes faith. We may be lavishly loved by another, but until we believe we're loved, that love is never really ours. Faith allows us to receive. Certainly we can understand this in light of the doctrine of the forgiveness of sins. Some may hear the truth of the gospel for years, but until they repent and have faith that this forgiveness is theirs, they do not receive it.

When were you forgiven? Was it when you said, "I think there is something to this"? Was it when you accepted the truth of the gospel as fact? Was it when you began to anticipate that you would one day be forgiven? Was it when you hoped God might forgive you? No. It was when you repented and said, "God has forgiven me now!" It was when you took God at his word and had faith that he would do what he said he'd do. When you reached out on the basis of the information you had, and believed that God did indeed forgive you, and began acting on that assumption, then you were saved. This is "saving faith."

> Our part is consecration and faith, and if we've done all we can, then we wait on the Lord to complete his part. But our waiting is not casual; it's active. Active seeking means we keep asking, we keep seeking, and we keep knocking.

So it is with "sanctifying faith." At the moment you say, "Fill me now," you can receive this work. When you reach out on the basis of the information you have and believe that God does indeed sanctify you now, it is then that he accomplishes his work in you. (Later we'll address the delay that God sometimes has in responding, but that can be the exception not the norm.)

When Jesus visited the city of Nazareth, he could do few mighty works. Why? Was it because he was not God anymore? Was it because God is not sovereign? Was it because Jesus was having a bad day? No. It was "because of their lack of faith." They could not believe that a local carpenter's son could do miracles. They did not believe it possible. And it wasn't possible! Because they could not believe it possible, Jesus could do no great miracle there. Can you see the connection with complete sanctification? Many doubt such a level of living is even possible. They couldn't believe it. How could such a thing be? Whole churches are like this. Like the people of Nazareth, they reinforce each other's doubt. Nobody believes! And sure enough, they're right. Because of the atmosphere of unbelief, God does no great sanctification among them. This describes much of the church today—even the so-called "holiness churches." So few believe God could make them pure that they feed on each others' unbelief. Sure enough, they are right—God does little among them because of their lack of faith.

Is this true of you? Is God's work in your life limited by your own little faith? If you doubt that you could be totally cleansed from your inclination to disobey, do you expect to be cleansed? If you doubt there is new power from God, you will likely turn out to be right—you'll not see this power. God's grace works in your life to the extent of your faith, and he is limited by the extent of your unbelief. If you believe he cleanses, he can cleanse. If you believe he energizes, he can energize. Your faith enables God's work within you. Do you believe God can fully sanctify you? Do you have faith that he will cleanse you? Empower you? Do you believe he could do it now? "So be it unto you . . . according to your faith."

"May God himself, the God of peace, sanctify you through and through . . . The one who calls you is faithful and he will do it" (1 Thess. 5:23–24).

But all this emphasis on faith in this chapter is not to say that God always responds immediately with entire sanctification as soon as you believe. He doesn't even save us always the moment we believe. Sometimes God waits. There are Christians who have totally consecrated all to Christ and who really believe God will sanctify them, yet he doesn't respond. We can't explain why God sometimes waits when we have done all we can, but sometimes he does. Some Christians sought for ten years before receiving this work (me). Others received God's work the moment they asked. God works in mysterious ways. We know this: our part is consecration and faith, and if we've done all we can, then we wait on the Lord to complete his part. But our waiting is not casual; it's active. Active seeking means we keep asking, we keep seeking, and we keep knocking. Many Christians have given up the quest for holiness because God didn't respond in ten minutes. Keep on seeking!

HOW TO KNOW 10
YOU'RE SANCTIFIED

How can you know that God has, in fact, entirely cleansed your heart? All that you've read so far in this book may seem biblical, logical, and understandable. But your real question may be, "Have I experienced this work? And if not, how will I know it if I do?"

You can know that God entirely sanctified you. You won't have to answer "I hope so" forever. While there is no perfect test that proves it, these questions will help you begin to answer the question, "Has this happened to me?

AM I TOTALLY CONSECRATED TO CHRIST?

Was there a time when you made a complete consecration to Jesus? Do you recall when you decided to submit to the Lord's will in every area of your life? Every area? Are you still completely surrendered to him? Perhaps this was a big event in your life, or it could have been the "final straw," but can you now say "I am totally his—I'm holding nothing back?"

THE BIG EVENT CONSECRATION

If you have a big event moment, it's likely still memorable to you. Perhaps you had been struggling against the Lord's will for many years, resisting his lordship in one or more areas of your life. You had lived in part-time victory and sensed little power from God. Finally, sick of your own uncooperative spirit, you finally surrendered everything to Christ. Maybe you "went to the altar" at a retreat or perhaps you surrendered at your bedside. Or it could have happened in your automobile or under a tree somewhere. But you remember as if it were yesterday. You "died out" to self and made a total surrender to Christ. You asked Christ to be the absolute master of all your life. In fact, right now, you can picture the place. Perhaps you even remember the date of your final abandonment to God's will. There was such joy and relief. To you, it was a monumental event of surrendering in your spiritual walk. Have you experienced a big event consecration like this?

> Can you say that right now you're totally submitted to Christ and you're totally committed to obey him in every way no matter the cost? Is Christ the master of your life? Can you say right now that there is no area of your life not under complete submission to Christ—you're holding nothing back?

THE FINAL STRAW CONSECRATION

Then again, maybe you've never had such a dramatic big event consecration. Perhaps the total surrender was less dramatic for you. Perhaps, for you, the final surrender came after many years of walking in the light. Sometimes you resisted the Lord's claims, but more often you obeyed him. Over time, one by one, you yielded to God particular attitudes, thoughts, or practices. And then one day you came down to a "final straw" area of commitment—the only thing left between you and God. You were totally committed to the Lord—except in this final area. "Yet, one thing you lack" seemed to be the Lord's words to you. And you did what you had done in all other areas—you yielded even this area to Christ. It was the "final straw"—you surrendered.

Regardless of which story is closer to your experience, can you say that right now you're totally submitted to Christ and you're totally committed to obey him in every way no matter the cost? Is Christ the master of your life? Can you say right now that there is no area of your life not under complete submission to Christ—you're holding nothing back?

DO I HAVE POWER OVER WILLFUL SIN?

Can you say that there is no willful disobedience in your life right now? Is there something God has clearly convicted you is wrong, yet you continue to do it? Or say it? Or think it? Is there anything God is specifically directing you to do, yet you are refusing to do it? Are you deciding to disobey the Lord in any area of your life? We are not speaking here of areas where you might fall short of absolute perfection, but we are talking about *purposeful* disobedience or unfaithfulness. If there is willful sin in your life, keep seeking God's power to cleanse and free you. But if you can honestly admit freedom from purposeful unfaithfulness against God, it's a sign of entire sanctification. Do you have that kind of power? Do you live that sort of life?

Can you frankly admit that you're obeying God in every area where he has clearly convicted you? This is the kind of power over sin that entire sanctification produces. This is the extent of the term *entire* in entire sanctification: entirely pure in desire to please Christ alone, entirely full of love for Christ, entire fidelity, and entire purity of intention. If so, it's a sign of entire sanctification. If not, why not linger here and seek God's freedom from the infidelity of purposeful sin? We cannot free ourselves from infidelity, but God has promised to do it, if we will seek his cleansing and power.

DO I HAVE LOVE OVERFLOWING IN MY HEART?

Has God changed your heart and filled it with love for God and others? Has God perfected your love so that your heart is full of love?

Perfect love is more than being cleansed from bitterness, grudges, malice, ill will, envy, hate, and other inward sins—though this happens in cleansing. Beyond this freedom, God can give you a baptism in love for himself and others. Not just loving likable people, but loving the unlikable, even your enemies? People may perturb you like they did Jesus, yet even when perturbed, do you love them still?

This love is more than a feeling. It's a mind-set, really a heart-set. It's saying, "I shall love others, for that is what the Lord wants me to do." It's active love, pursuing the best for others in every case. It's compassionate, selflessly committed to helping others without concern for personal return.

You may have not even noticed what happened to you right away. Then one day you realize that a particular bitterness you carried against someone has simply vanished. You recall the event where they harmed you, but your only response is love for them, not bitterness. Has that happened to you? Do you find yourself saying and doing things out of character for the old you? You perform acts and speak words of love for others that seem strange to your old self? Maybe you didn't even recognize this increase in love for several weeks or even months, but you can say today that your heart has been filled with love for God and others. This is not the sort of loving that you worked up or found by self-discipline but you got it from God?

> If there is willful sin in your life, keep seeking God's power to cleanse and free you. But if you can honestly admit freedom from purposeful unfaithfulness against God, it's a sign of entire sanctification.

The two greatest commandments aren't traps set by Christ to show you how bad you are. And they are not impossible commands of a merciless God. They are promises to his children—love God with all your heart, mind, strength, and soul, and love your neighbor as yourself. God has called you to love like this. Won't he give us the means to do what he called us to do? He will! Seek a baptism of his love to be able to fulfill your destiny—loving God and others completely. Can you honestly say right now your heart is full of love and this love came from God? If so, this is a sign of entire sanctification. If not, why not linger here and begin seeking that sort of baptism or filling of God's love.

IS OBEDIENCE THE CONSUMING PASSION OF MY HEART?

The following testimony helps explain what we mean by "consuming passion of my heart." This letter is written to answer the following question: "You say you're sanctified. Are you perfect?" "What a tough question, 'Am I perfect?' How can I answer it? If I say, 'Yes,' I set myself up as a target. Anything that looks questionable to anyone will be offered as evidence that I am indeed not perfect. But if I say 'no,' then it could be said that no work has then been done in me at all. So I shall answer you by saying 'yes and no.' Be patient. I'm not avoiding the question. Let me tell you what I mean.

> We cannot free ourselves from infidelity, but God has promised to do it, if we will seek his cleansing and power.

"I am not as perfect as Jesus Christ, the heavenly Father, the angels, Adam and Eve (before the fall), or even as perfect as I will be after death. I fall short of God's perfect standard of performance every day. And I still have a long way to become everything that God intends for me. In these ways I am not perfect. Yet, there are some ways where I could say 'yes.'

"First, let me say that John Wesley didn't like the word *perfect*. I don't either. There are better words to describe this life of obedience. The word *perfect* has an egotistical flavor to it. It sounds like something the Pharisees might say, which is quite the opposite of what sanctification is all about. *Perfect* gives most of us the impression that there is no need for growth or maturity, that everything is finished and complete. So I don't use the term myself. But, since you asked specifically, I will answer specifically. In what sense is an entirely sanctified person perfect?

"One windy March day, I settled the issue of Christ's control of my life and placed my total life in his hands. I decided that the

Lord would sit at the steering wheel of my life. That decision meant I would no longer run the affairs of my life for my own benefit, but let God be the driver of my life.

"I noticed several changes following this 'final wrestling match' with myself and the Lord. The greatest permanent change occurred in my heart. Ever since that day I have had a consuming passion to obey Christ. He has become the central force of my life. I have a new thirst for holiness and I want to obey Christ and Christ alone. In a sense, I am now a slave to Jesus Christ, like the 'love slave' in the Old Testament. I submitted completely to God in everything for all time and even for eternity. The issue was settled. When God responded to me, he filled me with a passion to obey him. I quit asking how much I could get away with and still be a Christian and started living for Christ as my supreme passion in life.

"I don't mean to suggest that I always feel on top of things or that I am constantly full of boundless energy. In fact, the feeling is not nearly as important as the set of my heart. I have made Christ the Lord of my life. No matter how I feel, I will obey him. I don't want to suggest that I always achieve the standard my heart desires. I still fall short of perfection but I do not fall short in my love and desire. I am not able to be as compassionate as Christ or as patient as Christ but I am 100 percent oriented to be that way. What I have is a new passion to be like Jesus. Holiness is not just a high priority for me; it's the central priority of my life around which all other priorities orient.

"This is the only perfection I testify to—a *perfection of intention*. I have a dominating hunger for holiness and I am filled with love for God. I hunger to be completely Christlike even when I fall short. And when I do fall short of absolute perfection I do not do so on purpose or in disobedience. Something happened to me two years ago this March that totally reoriented my priorities. Obedience to

Christ is now the central purpose of my life and I didn't work this up myself—God gave me this absorbing passion. To be like Jesus is the consuming passion of my heart."

This letter of testimony illustrates what we mean by *consuming passion for obedience* the Holy Spirit gives us in entire sanctification. Do you have an undivided heart? Can you say that your heart is totally magnetized toward Christ? Are you fully committed to obedience? Is Christ's will the central focus of your life? What do you want most out of life? Is it obedience to his will? Is obedience to Christ the consuming passion of your heart? If so, this is a sign of entire sanctification. If not, why not linger here and begin seeking a work from God that gives this gift to you?

DOES THE SPIRIT WITNESS TO MY HEART?

This final question is especially interesting. It's about the "witness of the Spirit" to your entire sanctification. You are probably familiar with this idea as it relates to conversion. How do you know that you are a Christian? There is the evidence, the promise of forgiveness, the fact of your repentance, and your changed life. But, there's more. Down deep inside you the Holy Spirit confirmed to your heart that he has adopted you into God's family. This is not a feeling; it's an inner certainty and conviction, not totally dissimilar to how you know you're in love. You just know it for sure, because you know it in your heart.

The witness of the Spirit to your entire sanctification is like this. You may have the hard evidence of your total consecration, you see new power over willful sin, you have experienced a fresh filling of love for God and others, and you have a consuming passion to obey Christ. But there is more. Somewhere along the line, the

Holy Spirit will witness to your heart that he has in fact done the work of entire sanctification. The Holy Spirit will eventually witness to your heart that it has happened. You will know it. This is the "witness of the Spirit."

This witness may not come immediately. It could be weeks, months, or even years before the Spirit convinces you of what God has already done. But the witness will come sooner or later. And the witness may not remain at the same intensity all the time. It may at times be stronger, and at other times weaker. But the Holy Spirit is faithful, and he will convince,

> If there is willful sin in your life, keep seeking God's power to cleanse and free you. But if you can honestly admit freedom from purposeful unfaithfulness against God, it's a sign of entire sanctification.

even re-convince, you of his work in your heart if you have been entire sanctified.

You can be sure, with a deep settled surety that God has filled you and cleansed you. His Spirit will sooner or later testify to your heart that he has done this work. Have you done your part? If you have done all you can, and you could answer affirmatively the questions above, yet you still do not have the Spirit's witness, wait on the Lord. Wait for his witness. Tarry. Seek his assurance. He will give you the witness of the Spirit that he has done this. Just wait!

CONCLUSION

How can you know that the Lord has done this marvelous work in you? First, you should examine the evidence:

- Have you made a total consecration to Christ?
- Do you have power over willful sin?
- Have you experienced a distinct increase in love for others?

- Is obedience the central focus of your life?
- Does the Spirit witness to your heart?

> The two greatest command-
> ments aren't traps set by
> Christ to show you how bad
> you are. And they are not
> impossible commands of a
> merciless God. They are
> promises to his children—love
> God with all your heart, mind,
> strength, and soul, and love
> your neighbor as yourself.

If your answer to these questions is "yes," you can likely say with assurance that the Lord has already entirely sanctified you. All praise to him!

However, if in being totally honest, you had to answer a question with, "This isn't true of me," then become an honest seeker. There is no use claiming something you don't have. In fact, this would bring you into greater danger. Rather, face these problem areas of sin and wait on the Lord. Ask yourself:

- Are there areas in my life not fully consecrated to the Lord? Why do I hold them back? Why not yield them now?
- Am I guilty of willfully disobeying the Lord against clear light he has given me? Why not confess my sin, repent, and turn away from that disobedient thought, word, or act right now?
- Do I possess bitterness, envy, ill will, malice, or an unforgiving spirit toward anyone else? Is my love weak? Why not confess these sins and turn away from them? If I have these attitudes, it's because I have chosen to have them; my will is the problem. Why not submit my will right now?
- Is my heart divided, partly pulling toward pleasing Christ, yet partly pulling toward myself and sin? Why not settle once and for all this matter of authority in my life? Why wait?
- Can I answer the first four questions affirmatively, yet I still have not received the witness in my heart that God has done

this work? If so, I need to wait patiently for his own good timing, all the while making sure I keep myself on the altar of total surrender.

Are you entirely sanctified? Baptized with the Holy Spirit? Filled—completely filled—with his Spirit? Is your heart full of love? These are all one work in the life of a Christian. Whatever one calls this second experience, certainly you hunger for a life of obedience and power, don't you? Do you believe it's possible? Can you believe it? Could God do a work in your life to make you be what you ought to be? Could God fill you with love? He can and he will! Seek and you shall find.

CONTINUAL CLEANSING 11

We who speak much about sanctification sometimes appear to emphasize the *event* of entire sanctification more than the process. Sometimes we even emphasize the event initiating holy living more than the holy life resulting from that event. This is unfortunate, for the sanctified *life* is what is most important. Of course, life needs an initiation, thus the emphasis on being cleansed instantaneously. But the continual life of holiness is the central issue in this book and of all good preachers and teachers of sanctification.

Take marriage, for example. Certainly the event of initiating marriage (the wedding) was an important instantaneous experience for me. I stood before several hundred witnesses in Stroudsburg, Pennsylvania, in 1967, and publicly proclaimed I was forsaking all others and taking Sharon as my wife. Our wedding was important—we have a whole book full of pictures of it. And when we first got married we showed our wedding pictures to every guest who came to our tiny apartment.

However, after a few years, our wedding pictures went into the hall closet, to be reviewed only when someone came by who had actually been in the wedding. Now, after more than forty years of marriage, I'm not really sure I could even find the pictures—I think they're in our memories trunk. Does this mean we no longer are married or the wedding day was not important? No. It means that our married life—walking together day by day—is more important to us than the event that started our married life together.

> The event (entire sanctification) is monumental. But the event initiates a new relationship. As the relationship grows, the event becomes less prominent and the life together is more important.

So it is with being saved or entirely sanctified. The event is monumental. But the event initiates a new relationship. As the relationship grows, the event becomes less prominent and the life together is more important. Holiness is as fresh as our last thought, word, deed, or motive.

Entire sanctification should not be viewed as something done "way back then" but should be a here-and-now experience that enables living in the trenches of real life. It's not a static life, as if we have arrived and are merely sitting around waiting to be taken to heaven. It's a life of active service to God and others. Holiness is not a final achievement, allowing us to rest in our completeness; it's expandable. Further spiritual growth invariably occurs. A person who is not growing is not fully sanctified. Sure, there are times of rest and assimilation, but invariably a fully sanctified person will be growing—on a constant journey toward complete Christlikeness. While an entirely sanctified person possesses the same *quality* of Christ's love, compassion, joy, peacefulness, humility, and patience, the *quantity* of these is still expandable.

The life of holiness is a daily walk with Christ. It's maintained by a continuous faith and consecration, which results in a continual cleansing by the Lord, our partner in this journey.

A sanctified person is not exempt from the battles of life, never to be tempted again. The life of holiness is not without difficulty, struggle, temptation, and even defeat. The difference is that these foes are encountered with a firm settling of will, "Not our will, but yours be done." And there is new energy to defeat temptation and serve God in Spirit-power.

SPIRITUAL DRYNESS

Do not misunderstand this book to suggest there will never be times of spiritual dryness. Could a sanctified person remain sanctified through a time when the enthusiasm, excitement, and the thrill has evaporated? By all means!

To say that a fully sanctified person would never experience spiritual dryness is to tell a lie. Almost every person testifying to sanctification will admit that there are times when God seems distant, daily study of the Word seems insipid, and church services leave them unmoved. What has happened? Is the work of sanctification lost? Some have thought so and gave up their confidence.

But such spiritual dryness can result from all kinds of causes. True, disobedience could be a cause. It's possible that God is urging us to move forward to a new area and we're resisting. This resistance to growth will promptly dry up the soul of a sanctified believer.

But there are other causes for dryness. A season of temptation can bring on a bout of spiritual dryness. We can experience an assault from the Tempter with such vengeance and for so long a season that our wrestling leaves us spiritually wrung out. We have little joy or excitement about anything. This kind of dryness is not sin but is to be expected in the life of total commitment. The Devil does not leave a fully sanctified person alone. He may redouble his assaults. These assaults can wear us out and produce spiritual dryness.

Another cause for dryness is *spiritual burnout*. It's possible to be so involved in church work, camps, retreats, evangelistic teams, counseling, and a dozen other spiritual activities that spiritual exhaustion results. Christian workers and counselors are especially prone to this malady.

Physical burnout can be another cause. A sanctified mother of three preschoolers, who is holding down a full-time job, carrying several responsibilities at church, and sleeping five hours per night will certainly be often tired and bored in church services. Her heart will not leap at the idea of giving another night of her week to whatever new program the church presents. This kind of dryness is common in the hectic world in which we live. A woman like this doesn't need to go to the altar, she needs to go to bed! Physical exhaustion can produce feelings of spiritual dryness.

But some of this has to do with *feeling* sanctified. The life of holiness is not based upon feelings. To be sure, this life has feelings associated with it just as marriage does. But reliance on feelings as the sign of our sanctification will eventually cause us to give up. What we call spiritual dryness can sometimes be a natural cycle of life. If it has been a general pattern of your life to be somewhat "blue" on Mondays, being totally filled with the Holy Spirit will not necessarily make all your Mondays bright and exciting. One man was troubled because every spring he became discontented and preoccupied and yearned to "quit the ministry and go live in Alaska." Only after reflection did he discover that during the first eleven years of his married life he had moved every single spring. His

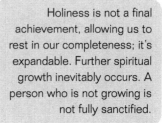

Holiness is not a final achievement, allowing us to rest in our completeness; it's expandable. Further spiritual growth inevitably occurs. A person who is not growing is not fully sanctified.

uneasiness was a result of this natural cycle of life, not because of his spiritual condition. Entire sanctification did not change his urge to do something different every spring.

It's important to determine the cause of spiritual dryness in the sanctified believer's life. If it's caused by willful resistance to the Lord, repentance is the only cure. But, if it's caused by physical or spiritual burnout, an assault of the Tempter, or a natural cycle of life, we should be careful to recognize the reason for our "dryness" and keep from casting away our confidence. All great saints of God experienced periods of spiritual dryness. But even if we are spiritually dry the sanctified life is not static—it continues by our continual consecration and faith and continues by God's continual filling and cleansing.

CONTINUAL CONSECRATION

We have said that to receive entire sanctification, total consecration is required. Likewise, to maintain this life, a continual consecration is necessary. At the event of our sanctification, we settled the question of "Who will be Lord?" but as each of us continues to walk with him, new areas will certainly arise where continued consecration is required. This continual consecration is made in light of the earlier, one-time submission of our wills to God. Marriage requires a total commitment, but the wedding vow does not exclude need for continual—even daily—recommitment. These fresh commitments are based on the earlier one-time event, but there will constantly be new ways to submit, love, cherish, and forsake all others.

> The life of holiness is a daily walk with Christ. It's maintained by a continuous faith and consecration, which results in a continual cleansing by the Lord, our partner in this journey.

This is the continuous walk of holiness. It's "walking in the light." Each time God moves his light forward, the sanctified believer obeys and grows. It's the natural expanding process of becoming more like Jesus. At the moment of entire consecration, the issue is settled. Our will is submitted completely to Jesus. Yet, there will be plenty of opportunities for us to reaffirm that initial commitment every time Christ nudges us forward. Making him the lord of our life at one moment must be followed by keeping him the lord of our life in daily obedience.

Thus, the sanctified life, most simply put, is the obedient life. It's the submissive life. It's a life where Jesus Christ is the daily leader, and we faithfully follow all of his prompting. It's a life of continuous growth and expansion as we obediently walk in the newly revealed light.

Where is God headed with us? Why does he bring "new light" to us in this walk? God is leading us toward Jesus. He is constantly at work in us, forming us into an image of his perfect Son. His light leads the sanctified person closer toward Christlikeness—in word, thought deed, and attitudes. If we're fully obedient to his leading, we will one day be like him, when we see him face-to-face. Until then, to the extent to which we will cooperate, he will transform us "from glory into glory." We cannot even imagine what he intends to develop in us in the future. But that need not matter. Our task is to surrender today, to obey today. Thus, the life of holiness is all about continual Spirit-powered obedience.

CONTINUAL FAITH

The faith by which we obtain the work of entire sanctification is not a one-time exercise either—it's a continual, daily faith. To receive entire sanctification, we each must come to the point of saying, "I believe God has cleansed me—the work is done and I claim it by faith." But to continue in this life, the same kind of faith is necessary. Continual faith is saying, "I am sanctified today because I believe God continues to cleanse me."

Once doubt sets in, the sanctified life begins to leak away. As long as we believe it's possible to live without willful sin, the possibility of full obedience is there. Once we begin to doubt the possibility, our life will eventually follow our doubts. Continuous faith to maintain the sanctified life is as necessary as initial faith to obtain it. If you're married, you understand this. The initial commitment you made at the wedding does not make for a loving growing life together. It's the daily and continual commitment and faith.

CONTINUAL FILLING

When asked why he constantly spoke about being filled with the Spirit, Dwight L. Moody responded succinctly, "I leak." We all leak. Though there is such a thing as being filled with the Spirit at one moment, this does not mean we do not need to be refilled. A sanctified person will be constantly seeking "fresh fillings" as preacher Virgil A. Mitchell used to put it. These fresh fillings maintain and reenergize the sanctified life of power and purity.

CONTINUAL CLEANSING

As we walk in this kind of obedience, Christ's blood keeps on cleansing us. From what? Weren't we cleansed once and for all? Christ's blood is a continued necessity for our daily walk. We will never reach a state of life when we no longer need Christ's atoning blood. Never! His blood continually cleanses the obedient believer as we walk in the light. We cannot receive a once-and-for-all cleansing then go our merry way in self-reliance. We must rely *daily* on the blood of Christ for continual cleansing. It's as we walk in the light that Christ's blood keeps cleansing us.

Cleansing us from what? We need his blood to cleanse us from the thousands of times we unknowingly fall short of his perfect standard. We need Christ's blood to continually cleanse us of every thought, attitude, word, or deed that doesn't edify and encourage, or in some other way falls short of absolute perfection, which we will never attain on earth. We need Christ's blood to cleanse us from the daily accumulation of "dust" we gather by traveling the roads of this world. We need the merit of Christ's blood to supply us with daily cleansing to maintain a life of holiness. This life is not self-maintained. It's maintained only as we are in a love relationship with the Vine, Christ Jesus. Holiness is living as Jesus Christ lived. Holiness is walking in step with Jesus. If we are to be holy, it will only be in relationship with Jesus Christ.

Mildred Wynkoop has illustrated this by asking readers to imagine themselves as suffering from defective kidneys and the only hope of surviving is to go to kidney dialysis several times a week. If your kidneys don't work, there is no hope in yourself; your blood supply is self-polluting. The only hope lies outside yourself. You must be attached periodically to a machine to cleanse your blood.

But suppose you could avoid the tiresome trip several times a week for dialysis. Suppose you could be attached somehow to a healthy friend, so that your friend's kidneys could cleanse your own self-polluting blood. Suppose that this friend was willing to be connected to you. As long as you stayed connected to this friend and walked step by step, your friend would insure a continuing perfection of your blood supply. Would you do this if it were your only hope in living? If you did, you'd have to develop an entirely different lifestyle wouldn't you? You'd have to go everywhere your friend went.

> We cannot receive a once-and-for-all cleansing and then go our merry way in self-reliance. We must rely *daily* on the blood of Christ for continual cleansing.

This is continual cleansing. It's being connected to Christ in a daily, obedient walk of submission and cleansing. It's walking where he walks. It's relying on Christ alone for cleansing. Such a life commences with a once-and-for-all yielding to his will. But it continues as we keep connected to Jesus Christ and walk in daily submission to his leading. Only as we stay at the side of Jesus, "walking as Jesus walked," are we able to maintain continual cleansing.

The sanctified life has a beginning—an event when we receive this work of God. But it's far more then a once-and-for-all event. The sanctified life is a practical daily life of love and obedience, lived by continual consecration and faith and continually receiving Christ's ongoing filling and cleansing.

UNDERSTANDING THE SANCTIFIED LIFE 12

Some have painted such an absurd picture of what it means to be sanctified completely that it has confused listeners and chased people away from seeking the experience. Others have the notion that this work of God transforms people into spiritual giants, raising them above all human frailty and even beyond temptation. They've even assumed that a fully sanctified person would live a life of constant emotional exultation and joy. This is poppycock—even Jesus would not measure up to these standards. Theologian Chris Bounds and I often chuckle to each other that our ministry is going about *lowering* the standard of holiness among such people. It's true that many often confuse absolute perfection with the perfection of love and intent.

To understand what we mean by a holy life (and what we don't mean) this chapter is written in a conversational style, using John Wesley's Q&A approach to these matters. Indeed many of the following answers are adapted from Wesley's own answers to similar questions. The rest of this chapter is based on a conversation between two individuals about the sanctified life. The first (Sam) has been a believer for eight years and a few months ago was completely filled with the Holy Spirit—"entirely sanctified" though he sought this experience for several months. Sam still has questions. The second person (John) is Sam's spiritual mentor. John has been walking in the sanctified life for many years. These conversations might help us better understand what the sanctified life is, and what it is not.

> The reason there is so little seeking for entire sanctification today is not just the lack of preaching on it, but because of the rarity of lay people testifying to this experience. If people never hear of a real healing they don't expect healing. If they never hear of a real person who experienced entire sanctification, they won't believe it's possible.

ABOUT TESTIFYING

Sam: It's been several months now since all this happened to me. I've told some of my close friends, but I'm not sure how much I should broadcast it. I almost wonder if sanctification is something like humility—once you claim it, you no longer have it. What do you think? Should I testify to entire sanctification? Isn't it too much like spiritual bragging?

John: Sure, you can talk about it, but be careful. You probably shouldn't talk about it to unbelievers at all. They don't have the spiritual perception to understand what you're talking about. And, yes, when speaking to other Christians, be careful to avoid spiritual boasting. When you testify to something like your own sanctification, talk humbly, making sure all the credit goes to God and you're not implying that you're better than others. Nevertheless, speak up. Why?—for two good reasons. First, it will confirm the experience to you. Just as public confession about conversion confirmed your salvation, so speaking up about God's second work of grace will confirm this experience to you. Second, talking about it will encourage other believers to keep seeking this deeper walk with God. The reason there is so little seeking for entire sanctification today is not just the lack of preaching on it, but because of the rarity of lay people testifying to this experience. If people never hear of a real healing they don't expect healing. If they never hear of a real person who experienced entire sanctification, they won't believe it's possible. When we hear about another's experience and the difference it made in their life, we can believe it could really happen to us too. So, certainly you should tell others. Just make sure you don't set yourself up as superior—set God up as the sanctifier. But speak of it for sure. Don't you think he deserves some credit for what he's done for you?

ABOUT TEMPTATION

Sam: OK, but I'm beginning to get confused on one particular point about this. I think I really need help on this one. Last month I was sure God had cleansed me. I could clearly tell the difference in my life. I am beginning to wonder about that now.

John: What makes you doubt?

Sam: Well, for a while, it seemed things were going well—I didn't even give the slightest consideration to some of the wrong thoughts and attitudes I had fought for years. It seemed like I would never even be tempted again. The power over sin was so strong. But as time passed, that changed. These last four weeks, I have been tempted severely to think the same kind of sinful thoughts as before I was filled with the Spirit. And I'm being tempted to pick up the very sinful attitudes God delivered me from. How could I be sanctified when I am tempted like this?

John: Have you given in to these temptations?

Sam: No, but they are as strong as ever—maybe stronger! Even when I resist them, they don't go away. It's like a giant battle, and I am getting shot at from all sides.

John: Why have you resisted so far?

Sam: I want to be obedient. I remember what I was like last year at this time, and I want no part of that defeated life. In fact, that's what's has me so bothered. I'm afraid I might give in and wind up worse then ever.

John: Don't worry so much. Be encouraged that you haven't given in to these temptations. You've committed yourself wholly to Christ, and the matter is settled—you have decided to obey him. God baptized you with his Spirit and has given you power to obey. Now you're resisting. God never promised you'd be free from temptation, just from sin—willful sin. There is no experience on earth that can place you beyond temptation. There may be periods of peace that remain for days, weeks, or even months, and certain temptations may lose their power but even these will be replaced by other temptations later on. You could be lulled into thinking you will no longer be tempted, but this is wrong. You will be tempted repeatedly. In fact, it's quite possible that Satan will double his attacks on a totally committed person. So, don't let temptation get you down. It's power to not yield to temptation that he promised you, not an exemption from the temptation itself. After all, a servant is not above his master. Jesus was tempted and so you will be too.

Sam: Then what was I cleansed from? If I am tempted by something, I must want to do it or it wouldn't be tempting. So how could I have been cleansed from my desire to disobey if I am still tempted to sin? If I'm tempted to sin, I must want to do it, right?

John: Whoops! Don't confuse temptation with the evil nature. What about Jesus? His nature was pure. Jesus was not carnal, but wholly committed to his Father. Yet, he was tempted in the wilderness for forty days. In the garden, the Devil even tempted him to avoid the cross. Did he want to be crucified? Was he saying to himself, *This is what I really want to do*? No. His humanness drew back from the painful experience before him. His natural, human inclination was to avoid pain. But there was still a struggle. In fact, he sweat as if with great drops of blood. Yet, the matter was settled from the start. His will was so completely committed that he could pray, "Not my will, but yours be done." His natural body resisted, but his heart was set toward total obedience to God.

When I'm tempted, I try to remember Jesus' example. He was without an evil inclination, yet he wrestled with temptation. Entire sanctification does not deliver you from human desires—fear of pain, desire for acceptance, sexual drive, and so forth. What does happen is the Holy Spirit cleanses your nature so that you are able to resist perverting these natural desires in disobedience. Your will is set. You have settled the matter of total obedience to God. God has given you power to resist. You love God enough to resist disobeying him. When great seasons of temptation come, you can know that the whole business is settled. When faced with temptation you can resist because the central prin-

> God never promised you'd be free from temptation, just from sin—willful sin. There is no experience on earth that can place you beyond temptation. So don't let temptation get you down. It's power to not yield to temptation that he promised you, not an exemption from the temptation itself.

ciple of your life is "not my will, but God's be done." The baptism with the Holy Spirit is not about removing temptation from your life. It's about enabling you to resist temptation.

ABOUT KEEPING SANCTIFIED

Sam: Alright. But what about staying sanctified? Like I said before, this life is so rich and different that sometimes I'm afraid I'll lose it. It's like I'm walking on water. I have this new power, but I'm afraid I'll lose it. Do you ever feel this way?

John: Sure. In fact, one time I did lose this walk with Christ.

Sam: How? When? How did you get back on track?

John: Well, it's a long and painful story. As you know, I settled this whole thing of Christ's lordship a while back. I had placed all of my life in Christ's hands. Eleven months later, I began to drift into casualness. The new zeal I had gotten began to fade, not suddenly, but gradually. I guess I began to take one or two things back off the altar of total consecration. They were areas that had troubled me before. I had surrendered them totally to God. But I started taking them back. The Spirit convicted me, but I didn't listen. Eventually I wound up in purposeful disobedience to the Lord—purposeful sin. Then my love began to dry up. I started becoming unconcerned and critical again. I lost the power I'd received when God sanctified me.

> Entire sanctification is like a wedding—where we give ourselves "entirely" to our spouse. But there is still a marriage to grow. The bride and groom may be totally committed to each other and filled with love yet there is still a lot of growing to do toward becoming a perfect husband or perfect wife.

Then I went to a renewal retreat in the mountains of Colorado, and the Lord made it clear to me what I was doing. I was simply resisting his will in my life. He and I both knew it. The blessing was gone. I was no longer completely his. I was no longer completely filled with his Spirit. The power had dissipated. That night, beside my bed in Colorado, I sobbed out my confession to God. I was resisting the Lord and I confessed it to him. That night I placed myself back up on the altar of consecration again and pled again for the power and love he had given be before. Within a day or so I sensed the power had returned.

I learned an important lesson through that painful time. Consecration is more than a once-and-for-all event. Keeping sanctified is done the same way we receive it. We keep sanctified by keeping our "all on the altar." We keep sanctified by keeping faith. It's a continuous act of consecration and a continuous life of faith. Can it be lost? Yes. In fact, many who claim to be entirely sanctified may have lost this blessing along the way, but their hard hearts keep them from admitting it. They still pretend to be living this life, but they aren't. These folk give holiness a bad name.

So, I'd suggest that you concentrate on keeping your all on his altar and keeping your faith in his continual cleansing and empowerment. You don't need to constantly worry about losing this life, but don't be too casual about it either. Perhaps your concern about losing this blessing is one of the major signs that you have it.

ABOUT GROWTH IN GRACE

Sam: You've said that the life of a fully sanctified person is not static or fixed, but is a life of growth. This makes sense to me, but I'm not sure I understand the vocabulary. For instance, how can I be more than entirely sanctified—how can there be anything more entire than *entire*?

John: You're right; the language is confusing. The *entire* or *complete* term applies mostly to being entirely consecrated and entirely filled with love. And it fits with power over sin—God can enable us to be "entirely" obedient. That is, we can have the power to live above purposeful rebellion. That's entire sanctification. But there's much more transformation to be done. There are many qualities he can build into us. Entire sanctification is like a wedding—where we give ourselves "entirely" to our spouse. But there is still a marriage to grow. The bride and groom may be totally committed to each other and filled with love yet there is still a lot of growing to do toward becoming a perfect husband or perfect wife. One can have perfect love yet still not be a perfect spouse. We can be completely faithful yet still not be completely perfect. This is where the growing comes in.

Sam: I sure have plenty of growing to do. In fact, I now think I fall short of perfect Christlikeness even far more than I used to.

John: Exactly! Entire sanctification cleanses us from our inclination to disobey and fills us with love for God and others yet it does not make us into angels. Purity of intention can come in a moment, maturity of living comes gradually.

The sanctified life is expandable, like the annual rings on a tree. A fourteen-year-old tree can be said to be a "perfect" tree. Yet, thirty years later it will have grown to be much larger, much stronger, and more mature—it will now have forty-four annual rings. A fourteen-year-old tree isn't supposed to have forty-four annual rings. Both can be "perfect" based on their age. Maturity is a relative matter. We can be pronounced "perfect" at an early age of our Christian maturity while there are still many annual rings of holiness the Lord wants to add to our lives as we grow.

The sanctified life is not a finished product. It's a life, a way of living. It's following the Bible's commands to "put on" compassion, kindness, humility, gentleness, patience, love, peace, self-control, and other qualities of Christlikeness. At entire sanctification, all this fruit of the Spirit-filled life is present. But our character is expandable. Our love, kindness, compassion, tenderness, insight, and patience can increase every day we're on this earth, perhaps even through all eternity. The life of holiness is expandable. In fact, we should grow more after this work is done. Why? Because now we're in total submission to his will for us and we're full of love.

ABOUT SELF-CONTROL

Sam: I want to change the subject a bit. Let's talk about self-control. I was reading in Galatians 5:22 the other day and one fruit of the Spirit is self-control. I have been talking mostly about being "Spirit-controlled." How is this different from being self-controlled? A friend says the idea of being Spirit-controlled sounds like people becoming spiritual robots. What's the connection between self-control and Spirit-control?

John: It's a cycle. The Spirit will not control anything in my life over my resistance. As I exercise self-control, submitting myself to the Spirit's control, he works in me to change me. As the Spirit moves

> The Spirit will not control anything in my life over my resistance. As I exercise self-control, submitting myself to the Spirit's control, he works in me to change me. As the Spirit moves through my life, the fruit of his work is self-control.

through my life, the fruit of his work is self-control. So they feed each other. The more I control myself, by submitting to Christ, the more he controls me, resulting in the fruit of more self-control. Like so many aspects of the Christian life, this is a partnership with God. As I continually submit to him, it gets easier to continue to submit to him. Submission and obedience come in greater and greater degrees. The result: continual growth in godliness.

ABOUT CAUTIONS

Sam: Since you have walked this way before me, could you give me some advice on living the obedient life? What are the dangers ahead? How can I preserve this life and make sure I don't lose it?

John: First, I would say *watch for pride*. You may have experienced such a dramatic change in your life that the Devil's best snare will be to encourage you to begin thinking of yourself as better than other believers—as one of God's best and most holy children. Avoid spiritual pride, whatever the cost. Continually give all the glory to God. Be careful of talking down to those who do not understand or who disagree with you on some point. I think one of the best definitions of humility is teachableness. Develop a spirit of teachableness. Don't assume you're always right and that everyone must now line up and become like you. Listen. Learn. Ask questions. Keep a spirit of humble meekness about your spiritual walk.

Some tend to think that their state of grace is so high that they are beyond the need of self-disciplined habits. Since they pray always, they need no particular time for prayer. Or, since "to the pure all things are pure," they can participate in questionable activities or read material of doubtful moral quality with no ill effects. Remember the Devil does not scratch you off his list when you're wholly sanctified. In fact, he may place you at the top of his list!

Sam: What else?

John: *Be careful of going off the deep end emotionally*. A person who is in total submission to God has a new spiritual sensitivity. However, you can run off on a tangent, supposing dreams, visions, impressions, prophecies, unknown languages, words of knowledge, or other ideas are from God. Sure, God will likely speak to the church through you more than before, but there is a great danger here of speaking for yourself and blaming God. Your own imagination—not God—could sometimes be the source. Down through history, when people have experienced this second work of grace, many have tended toward some sort of bizarre emotionalism. Be careful of this. Much damage has been done to the teaching of the doctrine of holiness by emotional extremism.

Sam: I recognize this sideline. I have an aunt who was just an average Christian. She got into a small group Bible study and received some sort of new special baptism, as she called it. She went right off the wall emotionally and finally wound up in all kinds of spiritism. She even tried to make contact with the spirits of the dead. So, I know I should avoid pride and extreme emotionalism. Is that it?

John: No, there are dozens of other bits of advice to those who are walking in total submission to Christ. One of the most important is to *continually strive for the disciplined life*. Some tend to think that their state of grace is so high that they are beyond the need of self-disciplined habits. Since they pray always, they need no particular time for prayer. Or, since "to the pure all things are pure," they can participate in questionable activities or read material of doubtful moral quality with no ill effects. Remember, the Devil does not scratch you off his list when you're wholly sanctified. In fact, he may place you at the top of his list!

There are a few others. For instance, *be especially on guard for sins of omission*—good things God prompts you to do which you're not doing. We can be disobedient to God as easily through purposefully not doing right as through willfully doing wrong. Prayerlessness is certainly such a sin.

And *be constantly on the watch against letting Jesus be pushed out of the center of your life*. Don't let anything begin to slip in and take dominance in your life. Nothing. Concentrate on continual consecration to the Lord. Keep obedience to Christ as the central goal of your life.

Keep your relationships with others in loving harmony. Never—absolutely never—break a relationship with another believer. Nothing will rob you of a sanctified life more quickly than a broken relationship with a brother or sister.

Finally, *live a model life in all respects.* Watch your example in spending money, in conversations with others, in sharing your faith, in how you dress and what you do, in your faithfulness in attending church services, and in serving the needy. Make sure everything you do and say will be an example of holiness and will bring honor to the cause of Christ. If you continually draw close to him, he will draw near to you and you will have even greater power as you become more like him.

This is the sanctified life—a life of obedience, power, surrender, and growth. It's a life worth living. And it's a life worth seeking.

SIDETRACKS 13 FROM HOLINESS

Many doctrines of the Bible are abused, misunderstood, or taken to the extreme in one way or another. While there is a main track for every doctrine, we humans have a tendency toward extremism, and thus solid doctrine frequently gets sidetracked.

This chapter traces some of the sidetracks from solid teaching on holiness. It's not done with any intention to be critical or cruel to any person or group. Rather, the purpose is to remind us of what we are not talking about when we speak of holiness. Many younger folk won't even understand this chapter, but it might warn them of future extremism to avoid. Some older folk who were raised in the Holiness movement will keenly recall some of these abuses. Some may exist even today. Every generation has had its holiness sidetracks. Here are some of the most common holiness sidetracks of the past.

LEGALISM

Some holiness people got off on the tangent of legalism. They came to identify holiness with "standards" and rules. In the most radical manifestations, the only way to be considered sanctified was to line up your life to their rulebook avoiding a lengthy list of "worldly" taboos. These rules were mostly unwritten, but all you had to do was look around to see what was expected of someone who was really sanctified. Many holiness people expected any serious Christian—and all sanctified folk—to line up with standards on hair length, hem-length, jewelry, makeup, and expectations about colorful or extravagant clothing. The list also included a variety of forbidden activities like attending dances or the theater, or even going bowling because these things were considered "worldly."

It's true: God requires entire consecration—a willingness to submit to God in all areas of our lives. However, we should avoid setting up our own tests of submission. If a whole group does this in concert, they're in danger of legalism. Legalism is not merely strict living—it's trusting rules for holiness instead of the atonement— that's why it's so dangerous.

Many of these standards were for women. While holiness males could dress pretty much like their coworkers, holiness women were expected to dress like their grandmothers. Among some holiness people it was commonly agreed that these standards were "the outward sign of the inward work." You could tell who was really sanctified by how they dressed and what they didn't do.

The trail of how this kind of holiness legalism develops is interesting. Whole denominations and movements can adopt certain taboos as outward signs of a holiness lifestyle. To show how such "standards" happen, we'll use women's hair as an example. There are few holiness people who still hold to this "hair standard" today, so it is easier to use here as an example. But you can substitute any of the more recent taboos and get the same results.

1. In the 1920's a new style emerged in the secular culture: "bobbed hair," cutting a woman's hair short. The new style was promoted by Hollywood film stars and was quickly adopted by the "flappers," a movement of young women who disdained conventional approaches to womanhood by shortening their skirts, wearing bold make-up, driving automobiles, smoking, dancing sexily, and insisting on their right to engage in casual sex. Christian woman and men were aghast. They rejected this "package" of values and likewise rejected some the social signs that came to represent them: make-up, dancing, short skirts, and bobbed hair (though not women driving automobiles). If secular women would make these things symbols of their sexual liberation, holiness women decided to steer clear of these symbols. They didn't want to be seen as a flapper and all that implied at the time.

2. Eventually some of these styles went mainstream and no longer meant what they had meant. Younger women came along who did not believe bobbed hair or make-up was advertising their sexual looseness, and they wanted to cut their hair and wear bold lipstick. Their mothers were aghast, still holding to the 1920's meaning of these symbols. There were churches full of woman who had rejected the flapper lifestyle and symbols, not just holiness churches, but most other churches too. Yet younger women pushed for bobbed hair, because they no longer believed short hair meant what it originally meant.

3. Preachers got into the act on the mother's side. First Corinthians 11:15 was often the basis of sermons on this issue. Since women were not to pray with their head uncovered (verse 5) and the hair was given for such a covering (verse 15), it was obvious to these preachers that bobbed hair was wrong for any woman who wanted to pray. Why cut off the glory God had given to a woman? Besides, the young women could just look around and see that every single woman in their church had long hair. Long hair became a test of being fully committed to following the clear teaching of the Bible.

> History is full of illustrations where the next generation after legalism is often lost altogether from the kingdom of God. Or, almost as bad, the next generation will totally reject any and all corporate standards of behavior, as they will head off on the opposite tangent of "license," preaching that anything goes when it comes to lifestyle and being like the world becomes a virtue!

4. Eventually a young woman (let's call her Lois) came to say, "This is absurd. I'll never let my hair grow out—not even to be entirely sanctified." Ouch! In her statement, Lois came to set up her own test of total submission. Her hair length became (by her own making) more important to her than submission to the Bible. She wouldn't submit to the hair-length rule. So she continued to bob her hair. Yet Lois was bothered by something lacking in her Christian life. She knew deep inside that complete cleansing had not occurred. Why? Her heart was not right. She established hair-length as a "no trespassing" sign in her life. Her problem was not necessarily her hair but her attitude: she was refusing to submit.

5. Finally, Lois tired of her part-time victory and life of mediocrity. She surrendered to God, "You can have all of me. My will is in total submission to yours. Now (assuming this was her final holdout issue), God responded to the completely surrendered Lois.

He filled her with the Holy Spirit, and she was cleansed and empowered. Lois experienced new victory and power in her life. What she did next caused trouble for the other young women.

6. Lois testified to her new found power, "I refused to let my hair grow in obedience to God because that seemed like a silly rule to me. I said I'd never give in. But, when I finally did, the Lord filled me with his Holy Spirit, and ever since, my life has been totally different."

7. Other young women in Lois' church heard her testimony and, like Lois thought, "This is absurd. I'll never let my hair grow out— not even to be entirely sanctified." Now they too set up the same no trespassing sign, and they too made hair length their own test of submission. They may rebel and walk away from church (many did) or stay around, but as long as they enshrined hair length as their own test of submission it became for them the test.

8. Eventually, you can see how a whole church full of women would emerge who agreed that a godly woman doesn't cut her hair. They together come to accept that a person can't be entirely sanctified if they have bobbed hair. Whatever we set up as a test to God, it becomes for us a test. Wherever we refuse, God prods until we surrender. Not because God particularly cares that much about hair or lipstick (or most of the other more current "things") but because God cares about our attitude of submission. In the time of the apostle Paul, the issue was eating meat purchased in the market that had been previously offered to idols. Paul declared that eating such meat was not wrong itself, however, those who believed it was wrong, thought so because for them it meant they were disobeying God (Rom. 14:23). Likewise, when everyone believed that short hair was wrong it became wrong for those who believed it was wrong—because the wrong was in the attitude of rebellion, not in the thing itself.

9. The whole business calcifies into legalism when a people come to believe these outward test issues are the price and proof of

the inward work. This is the way outward signs can gradually replace the real work of the Holy Spirit in legalism. When a group reaches this final step people begin to trust the rules for their holiness instead of trusting Christ. That's why legalism is so dangerous. In its advanced stages, it replaces the blood of Christ with human rules and thus becomes heresy.

It's true: God requires entire consecration—a willingness to submit to God in all areas of our lives. However, we should avoid setting up our own tests of submission. If a whole group does this in concert, they're in danger of legalism. Legalism is not merely strict living—it's trusting rules for holiness instead of the atonement—that is why it is so dangerous.

The greatest external consequence of legalism is how it hampers others from seeking holiness. These seekers stumble over false tests set up by "more mature Christians" (actually the apostle Paul considered them weaker Christians). Rather, we should place greater trust in the Holy Spirit to do his convicting work in the lives of believers. The Spirit will be faithful to point out to individuals their own particular areas of holdout.

But an even greater consequence of legalism may be the delayed results in the lives of the next generation. History is full of illustrations where the next generation after legalism is often lost altogether from the kingdom of God. Or, almost as bad, the next generation will totally reject any and all corporate standards of behavior, as they head off on the opposite tangent of "license," preaching that anything goes when it comes to lifestyle and being like the world becomes a virtue! This tangent is just as dangerous as legalism. Today, more people get off on the license sidetrack than into legalism, but both are dangerous sidetracks.

TWO-TRIP-ISM

For some, holiness has been watered down to a mere second trip to the altar. People on this tangent testify to "being saved and sanctified." They refer to two trips to the altar in their Christian life. True, entire sanctification, which is accomplished through the baptism with the Holy Spirit, is an epochal *event*. But to speak only of that event is a sidetrack from the main line. Two-trip-ism makes more of the second trip than the daily life of holiness. Holiness is walking as Jesus walked. When we treat sanctification merely as a second trip to the altar to get a second touch, we have departed from the Scripture.

When a church combines two-trip-ism with another sidetrack, holiness-or-hell, it causes many serious saints to dutifully take a second trip to the altar, even though they get nothing at all. This practice lulls these obedient church members into a false sense that they now have all they need. This encourages some preachers to be reluctant in calling for a decision on entire sanctification—they don't want their people to simply chalk up a second trip to the altar and count themselves sanctified when they aren't. Yes, there is an event side to entire sanctification—a specific time when we make a total consecration and reach out in faith to accept God's cleansing. But sanctification is more than a crisis event. It's a daily walk of obedience and love. Of course a trip to the altar is also a danger in the first work of grace too. Perhaps many "Christians" have not even been converted because they counted their one trip to the altar as their conversion when they haven't even been truly converted yet? Neither conversion nor sanctification is based on a trip to the altar—they're works

> Neither conversion nor sanctification is based on a trip to the altar—they're works of grace performed by God that change us completely. If there is no change, there was no sanctification—initial or entire.

of grace performed by God that change us completely. If there is no change, there was no sanctification—initial or entire.

HOLINESS CREEDALISM

Not many, but a few, have gone off on the tangent of holiness creedalism. They emphasize understanding and accepting correct holiness doctrine more than *experiencing* complete sanctification. "Protecting our heritage" becomes a fetish for them, and they are fastidious about checking out what new people believe about holiness. Creedalists may jealously claim they belong to the only true holiness group, and they reject as heresy any thought which disagrees with their firm position.

Holiness creedalism happens in many cases when a person discovers their daily life does not measure up to their doctrine. Their head is right, but their heart is wrong. The person's first inclination is to become a seeker, going on toward what he believes and what he once had. But that would require confessing need, something pride keeps them from doing.

Instead of seeking, they dwell on the head knowledge side of holiness, engaging in "preserving the doctrine" and engaging in hairsplitting debates, technical studies, and checking out others' beliefs on the subject. Holiness creedalists seldom testify to their own daily walk in holiness. They avoid descriptions of inner sin like pride, envy, jealousy, impure thoughts, selfish ambition, bitterness, holding grudges, malice, sinful anger, materialism, and self-will. They know too well that their heart is generously endowed with these vices. So they become more concerned with the doctrinal purity of others rather then their own heart purity.

While there are only a few holiness creedalists around today, we do see those who have reacted to them: those who say, "It doesn't really matter what you believe" or "We're all really saying the same thing anyway." Both are extremes: getting tied up in protecting the carefully manicured doctrine or ignoring the importance of sound doctrine altogether. Doctrine is important. However, we must go beyond right beliefs—to actually bring people into this life of obedience. Believing is important—but receiving is more important.

HOLINESS PIETISM

A few have left the main track and have retreated into holiness pietism. They emphasize prayer, Bible reading, total separation from worldliness, fasting, and other disciplines of the spiritual life. Like those who fled to medieval monasteries, they place the highest stake on being separate—a peculiar people, set apart from the world. The world doesn't touch them; they don't touch the world.

The work of entire sanctification has two sides to it: purity from sinful inclinations and power for evangelism and ministry to others. Those on the pietism sidetrack focus on the cleansing side. Thus, they become morbidly introspective, withdrawing from a needy world and boasting that their group is "small but pure." This was the great sidetrack of the last century among holiness folk.

However, during the current century, the error has been mostly in the opposite direction—to downplay the purity/separation side of the work and upgrade the power/presence in the world side.

Exactly how should a Christian relate in the world? Should the church be removed from the world—a peculiar people, different and separate? Or should the church be invisibly present in the world— not different, but mixed in and quietly influencing things for God?

Jesus described these two approaches to the world in the Sermon on the Mount. He taught us first that the Christian is to be light. Light is totally apart from darkness, unmixed with it in any way.

During the previous century, the holiness churches took a light approach. They considered themselves a "city set on a hill." Holiness churches acted like they were lighthouses, beaming out their message of warning. Anybody who wanted to join had to get out of the billowing waves of the world and come to the light. As they were rescued from the sinking sand, these new Christians became a part of a counter-culture church. Lots of emphasis was put on being strangers and "pilgrims" in the world. The light idea emphasizes separation from the world and being a counterculture Christian. The danger of this approach was that holiness pietists sometimes became so removed from the world that they hid their light under a bushel. Their lives may have been holy, but they were so separate from the world that the only folk who saw the light were the other Christians hiding under the bushel with them. Light was not meant for Christians to shine on each other, but to shine in a lost world. This is the besetting sin of the holiness pietist sidetrack.

However, during the current century, the holiness churches have mostly gone off on the other side of the road—toward the salt side of relationship to the world. Salt was not to be separate, but rather carefully rubbed into meat as a preservative until the salt itself was unrecognizable. This is the politically correct view in most holiness churches today. We're to be "in the world and not of it." We no longer want to be different or somehow considered separate from the world. We want to be assimilated into the world, to engage the world, to be absorbed as meat takes in salt. Our theory is that is how we can transform

> Both salt and light alone are sidetracks. The believer is to be both salt and light in the world—apart from the world: different, removed, separate, and, at the same time, in the world: assimilated, present, and quietly working to transform the world like yeast.

society—even change politics from the inside out. But there is a danger on the salt side too—becoming so assimilated into the world that the salt loses its savor. If the salt is no longer different from the world it makes little difference. This is the more recent danger in holiness churches. We have become so similar to the world that the unbeliever honestly says, "You're no different than us, you're out for the same life we are."

Both salt alone and light alone are sidetracks. The believer is to be both salt and light in the world—apart from the world: different, removed, separate, and, at the same time, in the world: assimilated, present, and quietly working to transform the world. Christians of every generation usually try to correct the imbalance of their parents' excesses then turn around and establish their own excesses. The balance, of course, is to be light and salt all at once. Or to use another metaphor of Jesus, we're to be yeast—in the dough of the world but quietly transforming the world toward God's kingdom from the inside out.

> Christians of every generation usually try to correct the imbalance of their parents' excesses then turn around and establish their own excesses. The balance is to be light and salt all at once.

THE MAIN TRACK

So what's the main track of holiness? How do we avoid the sidetracks? The main track of holiness keeps God's grace through Christ's atonement as the central focus of holiness and nothing else. Holiness is not what we don't do or what we abstain from wearing. It's not some special emotional feeling. It's not a mere second trip to the altar. It's more than a statement of doctrine, and it's not fleeing all contact with the world, as if being separate makes us holy. Holiness is Christlikeness. As long as Jesus Christ is the central thrust of holiness teaching, he will keep us from flying off on a tangent. Anything more than Jesus is extra.

HOLINESS AND GENDER 14
BY SHARON DRURY

Suzanne sat in her regular place last Sunday as Pastor Mike preached a powerful holiness message, calling his congregation to commit their all to Christ. He challenged the attendees to enter the sanctified life of service to others, putting off all concern for self. He especially emphasized overcoming ugly besetting sins such as lust, anger, pornography, hunger for power, and pride. Suzanne listened attentively and mentally examined her own life as he listed the sins: *Nope, nope, nope, nope, and nope.* She wasn't a proud woman, she

Sharon Drury is professor of Organizational Leadership at Indiana Wesleyan University and wife of Keith Drury.

just was being honest: none of these sins were her problems—and she could honestly say she was free of sin—at least these sins. However, her mind wandered to thinking about her husband and some of the Christian men she worked with and she found herself thinking of them, "Yep, yep, yep, yep, and yep—men really need this cleansing from God." Suzanne is sinning, but not the way Pastor Mike keeps mentioning. She needs sanctification just as much as her husband and the men she works with. Her sin problem is just different.

Women are not naturally more holy than men, but their temptations differ from those of men.

You may have noticed that the tilt of the other chapters in this book is biased toward a male perspective. This book was written by a male and that is a natural tilt. Writers write in the context of their own experience. This chapter is offered as a balance to what you might be thinking when you hear teaching and preaching on holy living that doesn't click for you as a female. Thus this chapter is written by a woman. However the chapter is also helpful to men, who likely (at least for now) do the majority of the preaching on holiness to both women and men.

THE HUMAN PREDICAMENT

Holiness deals with the human predicament of sinfulness. Entire sanctification offers hope to be delivered from willful sin in order to lead a life of obedience and love, as a complete and whole human being. We won't enter the debate here about biology and culture, but merely observe that for many women, the predicament of sinfulness appears different than for men. And since most of the writing and preaching on sin and holiness has been from a masculine perspective, a broader approach in this chapter—one that includes the woman's experience—should be helpful. Women sin too. Women are not naturally more holy than men, but their temptations often differ from those of men. This chapter describes how entire sanctification works out in the lives of many women differently than men.

But it would be ridiculous to make too much of these distinctions. We should remember that there is plenty of overlap between the genders, and the cultural roles of women and men are changing. So what is said here will also apply to some males and it will likewise make no sense at all to some women. And we don't want to pour any more guilt on women—we already have had enough of that. However, if the holiness message offers a route to overcoming sin and living in obedience, what does that look like for many women?

A MASCULINE APPROACH TO SIN

The first major questioning of gender differences in the human sinful predicament was raised by Valerie Saiving in 1960. Ever since, theologians and holiness scholars have pondered how a woman might experience victory over sin differently than a man—though much of this thinking has not filtered out in practical writing for ordinary women to read. For generations sinfulness has been defined mostly by males (as it has been so far in this book), and thus descriptions of the sanctified life tilt toward the male experience. Sinfulness has been usually defined as selfishness, self-assertion, the will-to-power, pride, exploitation, and treating people as objects instead of persons. Love (the opposite of sin) has therefore been defined as selflessness and self-sacrifice for the sake of others. This male oriented view of sin has so dominated Christian preaching and teaching that sanctification is almost invariably presented as surrendering self, sacrificing ego, crucifying the desire for power, and mortifying personal pride. The sanctified life is thus seen as dedicating oneself to the interest of others, being gentler, submissive, and even passive. But this approach presents a problem for women.

A FEMININE APPROACH TO SIN

For a variety of reasons, cultural and biological, many women tend to already live a life oriented to others. When women hear the usual-suspect list of sins, they get a free pass. They're being totally honest when they say they have always been this way. A call to surrender self and serve others, for many women, is to call them to do the very thing they are already doing and perhaps have done too much. Some women have so negated themselves and merged their lives into others that they hardly have a self. Many women have such low esteem that their self is nowhere available to surrender. Susan Nelson Dunfee described this as the "sin of hiding," which is opposite to the sin of pride and its antidote of self-sacrifice. Thus when women respond to the average male initiated call to sanctification, we presume we must already be sanctified, since we always have lived above these sorts of sins. Yet women face sinfulness just like men—our challenge is just somewhat different.

So what's the challenge for many women in hearing the message of holiness? It's often in gaining a full self to surrender and taking full responsibility as a self. Many women have negated self so much that we no longer have a self to surrender to God. The primary meaning many of us find is in identification with the lives of others. When the husband or children are joyful, sad, or pensive, we feel likewise, taking on the feelings of others, instead of being a self that is related to God apart from these relationships. Women are not inherently more "good" than males. Women are just as sinful, but in different ways. Valerie Saiving provided a valid list of the sins women are tempted toward: sins of distraction, diffuseness, triviality, sentimentality, avoiding responsibility, mistrusting reason, lacking centeredness, disrespect of boundaries, and passivity. These temptations seem trivial to males (and may even appear to males as virtues). But for women, they're sins just as much as lust, rage, and power-seeking. Women can be tempted to find their identity completely in others instead of God and are tempted to give their entire selves to others, leaving no self left to surrender to God. Some cannot love others as they do themselves, for they have no self to love.

> Many women tend to already live a life oriented to others. When women hear the usual-suspect list of sins, they get a free pass. They're being totally honest when they say they have always been this way. A call to surrender self and serve others, for many women, is to call them to do the very thing they are already doing and perhaps have done too much.

Tragically, this makes writing and speaking on holiness a tricky thing for males who are often our pastors. Males preach total self-abdication as the goal of consecration, while for many women it may be their major temptation—pouring out their lives for others instead of for God. Yet the experience of holiness is for women too, and women have sins to crucify just like men.

A FEMININE APPROACH TO CONSECRATION

So what does holiness look like for women, at least many women? Such complete consecration may not mean giving up self—it often means becoming a self. It might mean refusing any more to take our identity from having children or from our husbands or family. It could mean sacrificing "what others think of us" in order to find our identity in God alone. In consecration, she may have to put her boyfriend, her dream of marriage, her husband, or her children on the altar of sacrifice more than herself. She may need to sacrifice an identity that is wrapped up in family, kitchen, clothing, furniture, and friends and instead find her identity in Christ alone. Total consecration may mean surrendering her desire for passivity and peace and protection in order to enter the world to make a difference, instead of only being "supportive" of men who do these things. A woman still has an altar on which to sacrifice, but what she puts on that altar may differ considerably from what a man will put on it.

A FEMININE APPROACH TO HOLY LIVING

The resulting spirit-filled life for women may be less like the passive sweetness-meekness males preach about and include more powerful engagement in doing God's work in the world as a whole person. A sanctified woman will not shirk responsibility and hide behind the work of men. She will take full responsibility for God's calling and commands just like men do, and avoid constantly hiding in a helping role. The sanctified woman will enlist in God's life-changing work and she will be focused, undistracted, bold, and risk-taking for God. She will resist letting her ego be merged and blurred until it's swallowed up in the lives of others. Instead, she will come to stand as a whole, responsible person under God.

> Women can be tempted to find their identity completely in others instead of God and are tempted to give their entire selves to others, leaving no self to surrender to God.

Maybe you're thinking, "But this is unnatural for women." If you're thinking this, you're right—it is just as unnatural for women as it is unnatural for men to become tender-hearted, meek, humble, and easily entreated—all the things we expect from a sanctified man. God is not in the business of affirming our natural condition. He is able to do a supernatural work in us to make us into something unnatural to our flesh; this is sanctification.

PUTTING OFF AND PUTTING ON

In Ephesians 4 and Colossians 3, the apostle Paul talks about putting off evil actions and attitudes, and putting on the character of Christ. In both passages, he is telling us to act like the children of God. The problem of both doing and being is our need for a heart change—and since the temptations that so easily beset women differ from men, the route for a cure usually differs. For many men, holy living emphasizes *subtraction*—putting off impurity of thought and action. For many women, however, holiness involves *addition*, taking full responsibility and becoming a whole person under God alone. Again, this does not apply to all women, but it applies to many. The Christian character described in Scripture overrides sex and gender—but being a woman does not exempt us from responsibility.

WE NEED WOMEN LEADERS

The sin of hiding sometimes causes women to stay inside their homes, even after the children are no longer babies, where they idolize the family and immaculately care for the house—all in the guise of serving others. When sanctification is preached with a male bias, the sermon often pushes women further from the work God is calling them to and enshrines them in their hiding places. In the workplace, the sin of hiding sometimes causes women to defer to the men in the group to do the heavy lifting, to prepare for a leadership decision-making, and to be a servant of others for the common good.

For example, when women are needed in leadership positions in today's workplace, they must accept the responsibilities that go along with senior level positions. It involves taking responsibility for actions, taking criticism, and making tough decisions. Many women have been trained to hide and let the men take these responsibilities. Taking responsibility as a self often involves putting off the girlish desire for pleasing others, surrendering peer social status, or sacrificing a worry about what others think of us—often women's besetting sins. Taking such responsibility like this is hard for many women to do, but necessary in order to be a leader. God has gifted many women for leadership, just like he has gifted men. If God has gifted you for leadership, he will provide the strength and wisdom for it. This is why he is calling many women out of hiding. To resist God's call as a woman is sin, just like lust or pride or pornography.

Leadership also involves putting on a sense of humility and grace, because God has gifted you with skills that others recognize by appointing or electing you. Could it be that surrendering the sin of hiding might lead you to new work in the church or even a new career that comes with a sanctified sense of wholeness in body, soul, and spirit? Kristina LaCelle-Peterson has described how both males and females are created in the image of God, and he invites us all—both men and women—to do his work in the world. Sometimes that work involves accepting the heavy work of leading others, even leading men, and taking full responsibility before God for our decisions.

WE NEED WOMEN HOLINESS WRITERS

This single chapter is a poor excuse for an entire book on women and holiness, but it's a start. What we really need is more women to write on holiness from a feminine perspective. One recent book by Diane LeClerc, *Singleness of Heart: Gender and Holiness*, addresses this issue from a Wesleyan perspective, saying a woman's greatest sin is not the sin of pride, but the sin of hiding behind others, which she labels as "relational idolatry." A similar realization was the turning point in my own sanctification experience. When I quit hiding and surrendered the fear of "what others think," a whole new world of opportunity opened up that included a fruitful decade of Yokemates ministry with pastors wives, then earning a Ph.D., which led to teaching doctoral students. Worrying about what others would think of me was what I had to lay on the altar of surrender. This total consecration was not about thinking less or more of myself—it was to quit thinking so much about myself at all. We need more women to write on this subject from their own life experiences. Otherwise, when women read male-written books about holiness

> Complete consecration may not mean giving up self—it often means becoming a self.

we might think, *Well, I already live like that—this is something my husband needs.* But then half the population misses the message of this abundant life.

There have been a few good books on practical holiness in the past including *The Way of Holiness* by Phoebe Palmer and *The Christian's Secret of a Happy Life* by Hannah Whitall Smith, but these books are well over a hundred years old. Even though we have plenty of contemporary books on how women experience other aspects of life (women in the workplace, sports, travel), there are few published works about how women experience holiness. Maybe *you* should write this book on holiness. Would you consider that? Or do you shy away from such a thing, saying to yourself, "Who am I to write a book?" If so, could this be your own area of holdout from God? Is this what you need to lay on the altar? For women, entire sanctification often occurs when they quit hiding behind others and take full responsibility as persons under God alone.

WE NEED WOMEN PREACHERS TOO

When God created humans, he created them male and female. God has set up the world so that we cannot get into it without one male and one female. It was a good idea—not only for Eden, but for today as well. We need both genders to get a full-orbed approach to sin and sanctification (and everything else). When most of our theology, most of our books, and most of our preaching is done by males, we lose part of the truth. We need more women who will answer the call to preach to bring balance to the pulpit. Women in the pews need it. Men need it too.

> God has gifted many women for leadership, just like he gifts men. If God has gifted you for leadership, he will provide the strength and wisdom for it.

Women are not accessories. They are fully human selves and God calls females, just like he calls males, to do his work in the world. Too many demure, "Oh not me—I could never do that." But God does not call people without promising to equip them. If God is calling you, he will equip and empower you. Is he calling you to preach? Are you a young woman in college who can't decide on your future? Maybe God is calling you. Are you an empty nest woman wondering what you'll do beyond carrying around your grandchildren's pictures? Maybe God is calling you to preach. Have you been satisfied by letting men do all the preaching? If God is calling you, answer his call. Obey. Surrender to activism. It might be rough being a woman preacher and some will even reject your calling, but your hiding may be your own besetting sin. Come out and answer the call if you sense it. God knows what he's doing. This might be how God is calling you to holiness. How can you be totally surrendered if you say, "Me? Never!"? If you're hearing his call to preach, come out from hiding and obey. He knows what he's doing and his work in the world needs you too.

ONE WOMAN'S TESTIMONY

The tipping point of total surrender for women (and men) is often found at our besetting sin. Phoebe Palmer, the mother of the American Holiness Movement, found this to be so in her life. In chapter 10 of *Faith and Its Effects* (1848), Mrs. Palmer said that her final area of holdout was not in withholding herself, but holding out her family. She could surrender herself—even her life. But she was unable to fully surrender her family. These were her primary affections and she admitted idolizing her children. She also told of surrendering her friends and what they would think of her. When she was willing to give these up, she testified that an assurance of sanctification came. It was only then that she became fully whole in body, mind, and spirit. This was the experience of holiness she so long had sought.

Her life dramatically changed. She led the distribution of food, clothing, and medical supplies to the poor. Along with her husband, a medical doctor, they provided free medical care to the poor. Mrs. Palmer became the central figure in the 1850 establishment of the Settlement House in New York City's worst slums called Five Points, which led to hundreds of holiness missions across the nation in almost every urban city. Every woman who received this baptism of the Holy Spirit will not necessarily enter slums of New York, but she will enter somewhere. Holiness is not just to make us into pretty submissive wives; it's to rally troops to the front line of battle with evil and suffering, and women are not exempt from this draft.

WHAT ABOUT YOU?

The "women's temptations" in this chapter might not make sense to you. If so, don't worry, and re-read the rest of the book again. Quite certainly the route toward holy living and wholeness is not the same for all women. If you're a stay-at-home mom and have three preschoolers, you may be at a totally different stage for now. But hearing Phoebe Palmer's testimony still might be helpful. Holiness for her meant becoming a holy wife, mother, and social activist. So, if you are a woman reading this chapter, what are you holding back? What have you let get between you and God? Have you buried yourself in the lives of others so that you cannot give any "self" to God? Are you hiding behind others? Are you overly worried about what others might think of you? Have you been guilty of "relationship idolatry"? Is your life free of the sins the pastor usually lists, but you know your heart is still not right? What are you holding back? Listen to God's voice. He will guide you to surrender these. God loves you supremely and calls you to become all you were meant to be. He calls women to into the sanctified life too. The one who calls you is faithful, and he will do it.

A SANCTIFIED *CHURCH* 15

So far this book has dealt with personal holiness—a second work of God in the life of a Christian, purifying and empowering us for a life of love. This chapter is not about personal holiness, but corporate holiness—the holiness of a group, a holy church. Holiness is not just about making holy persons; it is also about making a holy people. Holiness churches should be just that—holiness churches, not just a collection of individual holy persons.

WHAT MAKES A HOLY CHURCH?

It seems reasonable to think that if every individual in a church were a holy person, then we'd have a holy church, but it doesn't work that way. "The whole is greater than the sum of the parts." One good man and one good woman do not automatically make a good marriage. Each might be a wonderful individual, but a wonderful marriage is more than two wonderful persons. Likewise a holy church is more than a collection of individuals who are holy persons. In fact, it may even be possible for holy individuals to come together as a church body, and then as a group act far less than holy.

GROUPS CAN SIN

We need only to turn to the Bible to understand this idea. Groups can sin as a group, and they can be righteous as a group. The nation of Israel was pronounced at times as righteous by God. But at other times they were collectively condemned. While some of this condemnation for sin was a result of God "adding up all the personal sins," in other cases it seems to be because God rejected the people as a whole—due to their collective national attitudes. A person can be arrogant and self-reliant, but so can a nation be arrogant and self-reliant. While an individual holds some personal responsibility for corporate sin, it's possible for the individual to be relatively innocent (personally), yet still the collective people are judged and the innocent suffer too. Every member of Achan's family was not guilty of avarice and disobedience, yet they all suffered. There certainly were at least a few good Jews in Israel when God punished them all and allowed the Babylonians to take them away into exile. God relates to individuals, but he also relates to groups of people—as a group—including families, tribes and nations. He relates to you and me personally, but he also relates to us as a group—and the primary group God relates to today is the church.

Churches can sin as a group even when there are many (perhaps all) in the church who personally do not willfully participate. Such corporate sins are often attitudes or sins of omission, but they can be detrimental to God's will for his church. When everybody is responsible, nobody feels responsible. So sometimes we stand back and allow the church to sin as a group while we personally do nothing. But we are responsible as

> Holiness is not just about making holy persons; it's also about making holy people. Holiness churches should be just that—holiness churches, not just a collection of individual holy persons.

a group—for God not only punishes sinning individuals, he punishes sinning groups. And when the church—as a group—sins, it is a serious matter.

GROUPS CAN BE HOLY

A group can also be holy—as a group. The church is supposed to be a holy people. In fact, a church can act Christlike as a group in a way that an individual cannot. Who would claim we are a perfect example of all the characteristics of Christlikeness? Who would say, "Here, look at me, and you will find a perfect example of Christ's mercy, grace, compassion, tenderness, justice, wisdom, and suffering?" Do you say this? Well, do you? See? Not one of us in our right minds would claim to be a perfect example of all these qualities of Christ. Yet in the church we can find them all. Not every one in the church exhibits all of these, but collectively we can find each of these attributes in the church. There may only be two or three people who represent Christlike compassion fully, but you can find them in the church. There might only be a single person who is suffering at Christlike levels, but you can find them in the church. It's in the church that we find Christlikeness in its fullest sense. This is why we never consider ourselves individually the "body of Christ." Would you? Never! I am not the body of Christ. Neither are you. We are the body of Christ—all of us in the church collectively. Together we can find among us all the character qualities of Jesus Christ. While none of us perfectly exhibits all of these qualities, together in the power of the Spirit we show the world what Jesus is like—we are the only body of Christ they can see.

OUR INDIVIDUALISTIC MIND-SET

Every cell of our Western individualistic minds rebels at this idea. Our culture trains us from childhood to refuse to melt—to become a stand-alone individual. Television and movies lionize individuals who claim, "I did it my way." The theater constantly throws at us heroes who buck the system, ignore the group, and live by their own standards. We are discipled by our culture to demand our own rights, get what we want, and make our desires known, as angry customers who will threaten to take our business elsewhere if our demands are not met. This is how we're raised—especially in North America. It leaks into our religion as well, for

> Churches can sin as a group even when there are many (perhaps all) in the church who personally do not willfully participate.

it is difficult to have a religion that departs too far from the culture's values. This is why we come to worship like customers insisting on having the meal served exactly to our liking.

So we have personal devotions, personal mentoring, and personal time alone with God as we elevate the privatization of religion and marginalize the corporate church. One popular student Facebook group on a Christian college campus is named "We love Jesus, but hate the church." What kind of Christians are these? Yet these students merely took the privatized personalized religion of their parents to its logical end. When personal devotions become more important than corporate worship; personal deeds become more important than the church's group service; private time with God is elevated, while the Christ-established sacraments at church are dismissed, this is what we get a generation later: people who claim to love Jesus and hate his body.

But it can't be done. We can't behead Jesus and reject his body. There are no real Christians who hate the church. How can someone love Christ whom they have not seen, if they do not love his body that they can see?

ONE HOLY CHURCH

So, just as groups can sin, they also can be holy as a group. Some churches are holy, and others are not. Is your church a holy church? If not, it can be. Indeed the New Testament continually urges the church to be holy. It calls us collectively to be sanctified and purified. In our individualized culture we have difficulty reading the Bible for what it really says. We read our own assumptions into the Bible. For instance, when the Bible says, "You be holy," we immediately take the "you" to mean me—me personally. In our language, "you" can be taken either as singular or plural, but we almost always take the Bible's "you's" as singular—to me personally. Yet in the Bible, most all the commands to be holy are plural—plural instructions to the church as a group—as in, "y'all be holy." How holiness churches have missed this emphasis for so long escapes us, but it is clearly the teaching of Scripture. God wants a holy people, and he won't get it just by making holy individuals; there is a sanctification he wants to do of the church collectively too.

HOW CAN A CHURCH BECOME HOLY?

Most of us understand the idea of corporate sin easier than corporate holiness, but just as groups can sin, groups can be holy. So what is holiness? It's Christlike living in word, thought, deed and attitude. It's living as Jesus would live, relying on the power of the Holy Spirit. Holiness is loving others, serving others, worshiping God, being easily entreated, hungering for more of God, avoiding disobedience, reaching out to the lost, the poor, and those in need. All of these things an individual can do—but so can a group. Your church can be a holy church. How? By doing all these things together as a group. Obviously just gathering as a congregation does not make the group holy, any more than attending church makes an individual holy.

So how does God sanctify the church—the group? He sanctifies the church through the various "means of grace." The means of grace are the channels of changing grace God uses to make us holy. God uses the means of grace to mold his church, to correct her, to eliminate sin and foot-dragging, to grant us a collective passion for the lost, and to enable us to love him, each other, and the world.

There are two categories of the means of grace—personal and corporate. Some means of grace are personal, like solitude and silence. However, other means of grace can only be received corporately, like the Lord's Supper. Still other means fall into both the personal and corporate categories—like prayer. Just as God uses personal devotions to change us individually, he uses the corporate means of grace to change the church corporately into his Son's image.

But it is not by the means of grace alone that God changes his church, for there are corporate experiences that also can change the corporate soul of a church. For instance, a church can be filled with the Holy Spirit just like an individual can be filled. And we are speaking here of more than simultaneous individual fillings—God will sometimes indwell the collective "body of Christ" in the way he has indwelt individuals. So there are both the corporate means of grace and corporate experiences that can sanctify a church making it one holy church. Thus, to consider how God sanctifies the church, we must look at the corporate means God uses to make a holy church.

Filling with the Holy Spirit. We're familiar with being personally filled with the Spirit, but few of us ever expect (or even believe) that the whole church could be filled with the Spirit. But what if we could experience this today? What if God came upon his gathered people and filled the gathered people with the Spirit. What would that be like? Well, it would be like the church in the book of Acts. When

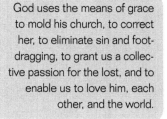

God uses the means of grace to mold his church, to correct her, to eliminate sin and foot-dragging, to grant us a collective passion for the lost, and to enable us to love him, each other, and the world.

God fills his church with the Holy Spirit, that body will never be the same again. Why does this not happen today? Why is such an experience not even sought or expected? We give altar calls for individuals to be Spirit-filled, but what if an entire congregation at once sought this experience—as a church? What if we all went to the altar as a church? Did God quit filling the church with the Spirit after Acts 2? Some of us don't think so.

But most of our churches will never be Spirit-filled. Why? We only imagine that if each individual were filled with the Spirit, then when we all gather, the church itself would automatically be Spirit-filled. Thus we don't even believe there is such a thing as the Spirit filling a church like God did at Pentecost. In our unbelief, we get exactly what we expect—we expect nothing and get nothing. If we want our church to be a sanctified church, we need to help each other believe there is such a thing as a corporate Spirit-filling from God. Then we need to seek it—seek to be filled with God's Spirit, as a church.

It's hard to even imagine, isn't it? We have so individualized and personalized the work of God, we can barely even conceive of corporate sanctification. But God would be pleased to respond to such a seeking church. He might just fill our entire collective church with the Holy Spirit at once, while we are all gathered at one place at one time. Boy! If he did, what would that be like? Well, it would be like the New Testament church.

Moving of God. Maybe it's easier for us to imagine a "moving of God" than a corporate filling of the Spirit. Have you ever been in a service where God moved? Such a thing happened when they dedicated the Tabernacle in the Old Testament. It happened again later at the Temple dedication. Has it ever happened at your church? Have you ever seen the Spirit of God descend upon his church in a way that was undeniable and indelible? Maybe it happened during the music or maybe during the preaching or an altar call, but have you ever seen God's moving that could not be attributed to human manipulation or emotion? Such an experience changes a congregation for years. When God moves among his people, they change. Not just as individuals (though that is also true), but collectively the church becomes closer to God. Some churches have to go back a long way in their history to cite a memory of God's moving. How far back does your church have to go?

The Lord's Supper. While revivalist holiness people can recall things like God's "moving," we often have a poorer record on the actual sacraments—the means of grace established by Christ himself. Communion is more than a remembrance service for a dead man—it is a means of grace designed by God to change his church and make her holy. John Wesley fought the lackadaisical attitude toward the Lord's Supper in his day, and we must fight it today. We think communion "takes too long" or "isn't relevant to daily life" or "it is a downer and we want brighter services." So we assign it to some sideshow service that most people can skip. Shame on us! No wonder the church lacks holiness—it lacks one of the chief means of grace, the Lord's Supper. When John Wesley was asked, "How often should I take communion?" he responded simply, "As often as you can." We argue that it loses meaning if we "have it too often," yet we would not say this of prayer—"let's pray less or it will lose its meaning." Would we be willing to read Scripture only once a quarter to make sure it "doesn't lose its meaning?" The Lord's Supper is a mystical gift from God to his church in order to sanctify the body. It cannot be practiced by an individual any more than marriage can be experienced by only one person. It's a group experience and a group-sanctifying experience, if we will let it become that. God intends to sanctify his church through his blood and body. If we will commune often and commune by faith, God will change us as a corporate body to become a church more like Christ. Can we take communion more frequently? Will we take it believing in God's changing power through this sacrament? If we will, he will.

Conversion and Baptism. Seeing new converts come to Christ in our church and receiving them into the family through the sacrament of baptism is a transforming experience for a church. Too many churches have seen too many months go by without seeing a single person converted and changed and receiving baptism. When a church sees a life changed, the church is changed. We are reminded, "This is what it's all about." We become a more godly church—a church that values the things God values. Too many churches are practicing spiritual birth control—they have gone for months, even years—without seeing a new birth in the family. When we witness new births consummated in the sacrament of baptism it is a means of grace to us corporately.

Testimony. Hearing God's mighty works in the lives of his people is a means of grace that God uses to sanctify us as a church. Whether it is the old fashioned personal testimony or the more modern edition of projected testimonies by video, God uses these testimonies to make us holy. Without such a witness, our church will gradually forget God's power to deliver people from their sinful habits. A miraculous deliverance is a wonderful thing, but if nobody hears about it at church, it is no more useful to the church than a tree falling in the woods with nobody around to hear it.

Corporate Prayer. Just as prayer is a significant personal means of grace, it is also a collective means of grace by which God sanctifies the church. In prayer, we're melted together as one church and we learn to "wait on the Lord," listening for his direction and commands. A church that uses prayer as a segue, just to provide cover for those on the "stage" to move to a new location, will not become a holy people. Prayer is more than an oil to make the minute-by-minute worship schedule work smoothly. It's a face-to-face encounter with God. Prayer is the church's means of approaching his throne together to lay before him our collective requests and to receive prompts. The church that prays together stays together. And the church that prays together becomes more like Christ every time it does so. It's a means of grace through which God sanctifies the church. A church that takes prayer so lightly can no more be holy than an individual who prays that way.

Scripture. It takes very little effort to convince Protestants of the importance of Scripture. In some ways we consider Scripture to be a greater sacrament than the actual sacraments. We treat it as the chief means of grace no matter what we say in our doctrine. We may be right or wrong in this revisionist approach, but we certainly will agree that when God's people are gathered, the public reading of Scripture and scriptural preaching is a means of grace for God to make his church collectively a holy people. Reading the Bible on our own at home is important, but listening to the Scripture read and preached at church is even more important. Scripture has a cleansing effect on the gathered people of God, beyond what it has when we read it by ourselves. While protestants may do better at understanding the importance of Scripture as a means of grace, we still fall short in understanding how it is a corporate means—how God uses the Scriptures to sanctify the church as we hear it read and preached. If we don't upgrade the reading of Scripture in our church worship services, our claims about the value we put in Scripture is but a sounding gong.

Koinonia. Pot-luck suppers and traveling in a van to shop on a Saturday may seem like mostly fun, but they are an essential corporate means of grace through which God sanctifies his church. How can we love each other if we are seldom together? "Doing life together" is an increasing theme in the emerging church, and it is sound doctrine. God sanctifies his church as we mix together. Steve DeNeff reminds us that the church is like God's washing machine. We all come together and tumble in the washing of the word as we experience a group cleansing. *Koininia* denotes more than fellowship, but just getting together is a start. As we gather and "do life together," God uses us to encourage, correct, urge, guide, and inspire each other. From our interaction, we come away encouraged, corrected, urged, and inspired. As we gather together, he is in the midst of us, helping us become more like Christ together. As we do this, we become in actuality what we are in name: the community of Christ.

> We need to help each other believe there is such a thing as a corporate Spirit-filling from God. Then we need to seek it—seek to be filled with God's Spirit, as a church.

These are just a few of the "corporate means of grace" by which God sanctifies his people as a group. These are enough to awaken us to the idea of a church becoming a holy church together. God wants to turn the gathered assembly of individuals who show up to "get something personally" into a people of God, who live and serve together and show the world what the body of Christ looks like. It looks like a group—a holy group.

> None of us personally can be his bride nor should we even want to be. But all of us together are the bride of Christ.

All this talk about corporate sanctification may seem strange in a book mostly about personal holiness. But it's true and it's biblical. While personal holiness is very important it's not enough—God wants a holy people, not just holy persons. Once we see that our stubborn individuality is a barrier to "letting go and letting God" work to make his gathered church a holy people, we can start this collective journey together. Maybe we can start to see our church like God sees it—as his chosen bride who is being made perfect by the groom. None of us personally can be his bride nor should we even want to be. But all of us together are the bride of Christ. Together he wants to cleanse us to make us his radiant bride "without spot or wrinkle." He does this as we are together. God will make us one holy church, if we will let him. When a church—as a church—seeks God's sanctification, it can experience a work of grace together that makes the group a holy church.

For a detailed exploration of the corporate means of grace, see the book *There is No "I" in Church* by Keith Drury.

PERSONAL TESTIMONIES 16

How do we know a doctrine is true? How can we decide if what this book says about entire sanctification and the baptism with the Holy Spirit is truth?

First and last we must ask if this is biblical. To be sure, there are varied interpretations of the Bible, but the testing of a doctrine begins and ends with the Bible. The question to ask is "Does the Bible teach sanctification?"

Second, we can ask how does this fit with reason? God does not expect us to turn off our minds when studying doctrine. God has created us with an intellect, and he expects us to use it in understanding doctrine. I once heard a famous seminar leader say, "If you want to know what God wants you to do, just use your human logic . . . then do the opposite." His argument was that God's ways are never logical to the human mind. This is silliness. The Bible is our starting point, but we are expected to ask questions of reason as we formulate Christian doctrine. After determining that sanctification is biblical, the next task is to apply our intellect to the Bible's teaching to come up with a reasonable and consistent doctrine. This book has tried to be reasonable in presenting these claims.

Third, we can ask, how does this doctrine fit with church tradition? This is not to say that the church's doctrine must never change. If that were true, we would never have had the Protestant Reformation. However, we cannot simply invent new doctrines on a whim. If the strain of holiness and sanctification does not go all the way back to the apostles and is not represented throughout some of church history, then the doctrine is of dubious value, maybe even completely false. If it is completely new, it is not true. If it is true, it is not completely new. We have tried to present holiness in this book rooted in history—it is not a new idea.

Finally, we can ask, how does this doctrine play out in experience? That is, has anybody ever found this to be true in their own life? Is there any experiential evidence that this doctrine works? Now, of course, there is a danger here. Experience alone can't validate a doctrine. The world is full of people with wacky experiences. Neither can reason alone, nor tradition alone, accredit doctrine. That's why we must start and finish with the Bible. The Bible is like home plate—we start there, then tag reason, tradition, and experience before coming back to the Bible itself. But, experience is an important third base. Does the doctrine work? Does it fit with human experience? Has anyone ever experienced the

Spirit-baptism described in this book? Are there real people who have been entirely sanctified? Completely filled with the Holy Spirit? Cleansed and empowered to live above willful sin? Are there testimonies from people like this?

This chapter is dedicated to such testimonies. As you read each testimony, allow God to speak to you. We've studied the Bible. We've attempted to apply our reason to these truths. We've traced the holiness message in the Word and down through history. Now we should read the personal testimonies of some individuals. We could use mostly current people, but we have chosen mostly to root around in history and find testimonies to this deeper life. Enjoy their personal testimonies and see if they ring true.

TESTIMONY OF CATHERINE BOOTH

Catherine Booth (1829–1890) was the co-founder of the Salvation Army. She testified, "I struggled through the day, until a little after six in the evening, when William joined me in prayer. We had a blessed season. While he was saying, 'Lord, we open our hearts to receive Thee,' that word was spoken to my soul: 'Behold, I stand at the door and knock. If any man hear my voice, and open unto me, I will come in and sup with him.' I felt sure He had been knocking, and oh, how I yearned to receive him as a perfect Saviour! But oh, the inveterate habit of unbelief! How wonderful that God should have borne so long with me.

"When we got up from our knees, I lay on the sofa, exhausted with the effort and excitement of the day. William said, 'Don't you lay all on the altar?' I replied, 'I am sure I do!' Then he said, 'And isn't the altar holy?' I replied in the language of the Holy Ghost, 'The altar is most holy, and whatsoever toucheth it is holy.' Then said he, 'Are you not holy?' I replied with my heart full of emotion and with some faith, 'Oh I think I am.' Immediately the word was given me to confirm my faith, 'Now are ye clean through the word I have spoken unto you.' And I took hold—true, with a trembling hand, and not unmolested by the tempter, but I held fast the beginning of my confidence, and it grew stronger, and from that moment I have dared to reckon myself dead indeed unto sin, but alive unto God through Jesus Christ, my Lord."

From a letter by Catherine Booth to her parents, cited by
James Gilchrist Lawson, *Deeper Experiences of Famous Christians.*
(Anderson, Ind.: Warner Press, 1978), pp. 255–56.

THE TESTIMONY OF DAVID BRAINERD

David Brainerd (1718–1747) was a fervent American missionary to the Native Americans. He testified, "In the morning, I felt my soul *hungering and thirsting after righteousness.* In the forenoon, while I was looking on the sacramental elements, and thinking that Jesus Christ would soon be 'Set forth crucified before me,' my soul was filled with light and love, so that I was almost in an ecstasy; my body was so weak I could hardly stand. I felt at the same time an exceeding tenderness and most fervent love towards all mankind; so that my soul, and all the powers of it seemed, as it were, to melt into softness and sweetness. This love and joy cast out fear, and my soul longed for perfect grace and glory.

"I felt exceeding dead to the world and all its enjoyments: and yet then had as much comfort of life as almost ever I had. Life itself appeared but an empty bubble—the riches, honors, and enjoyments of it extremely tasteless. I longed to be entirely *crucified* to all things here below. My soul was sweetly resigned to God's disposal of me; and I saw there had nothing happened to me but what was best for me . . . It was my meat and drink to be holy, to live to the Lord, and die to the Lord. And I then enjoyed such a heaven, as far exceeded the most sublime conceptions of an unregenerate soul, and even unspeakably beyond what I myself could conceive at another time."

From his journal entries of October 19, 1740, and March 10, 1743,
cited by Lawson, *Deeper Experiences*, pp. 264–65.

THE TESTIMONY OF WILLIAM BRAMWELL

William Bramwell (1759–1818) was the most significant revivalist and holiness evangelist in Methodism after John Wesley's death. He testified, "When in the house of a friend at Liverpool, whither I had gone to settle some temporal affairs, previously to my going out to travel, while I was sitting, as it might be, on this chair [pointing to his chair], with my mind engaged in various meditations concerning my present affairs and future prospects, my heart now and then lifted up to God, but not particularly about this blessing, *heaven came down to earth*; it came to my soul. The Lord, for whom I had waited, came suddenly to the temple of my heart; and I had an immediate evidence that this was the blessing I had for some time been seeking. My soul was then all wonder, love, and praise."

Cited by Oswald J. Smith, *The Enduement of Power.*
(London: Marshall, Morgan & Scott, 1933), p. 59.

THE TESTIMONY OF J. WILBUR CHAPMAN

J. Wilbur Chapman (1859–1918) was an American evangelist, revivalist, and pastor. He testified, "One incident connected with my own Christian experience can never be effaced from my memory. I was seated in my country home reading the accounts of the Northfield conferences, before I had even thought of attending the same, when one sentence in an address delivered by Mr. Meyer arrested my attention. It was concerning the life of surrender, and the sentence was as follows: 'If you are not willing to give up everything to God, then can you say, *I am willing to be made willing?*' It was like a star in the midnight darkness of my life and led to a definite surrender of myself in October 1892. But after that, there were still some discouragements and times of depression, and, standing one morning very early in front of Mr. Moody's house with the Rev. F. B. Meyer, I said to him, 'Mr. Meyer, what is my difficulty?' I told him of my definite surrender and pointed out to him my times of weakness and discouragement, and, in a way which is peculiar to himself, he made answer, 'My brother, your difficulty is doubtless the same as the one I met. Have you ever tried to breathe out six times without breathing in once?' Thoughtlessly I tried to do it, and then learned that one never breathes out until he breathes in, that his breathing out is in proportion to his breathing in, that he makes his effort to breathe in and none to breath out. Taking my hand in his, my distinguished friend said, 'It is just so in one's Christian life, we must be constantly breathing in of God, or we shall fail,' and he turned to make his way to Mr. Moody's house for breakfast while I hastened up to my room in Weston Hall, thanking God that I had a message better to me than any sermon I had ever heard."

J. Wilbur Chapman, *The Life and Work of Dwight L. Moody.* (New Haven, Conn.: Butler & Alger, 1900), pp. 199–200.

THE TESTIMONY OF
CHARLES GRANDISON FINNEY

Charles Grandison Finney (1792–1875) was a minister of the gospel who was a key figure in the Second Great Awakening in America. He testified, "As I turned and was about to take a seat by the fire, I received a mighty baptism of the Holy Ghost. Without any expectation of it, without ever having the thought in my mind that there was any such thing for me, without any recollection that I had ever heard the thing mentioned by any person in the world, the Holy Spirit descended upon me in a manner that seemed to go through me, body and soul. I could feel the impression, like a wave of electricity going through and through me. Indeed it seemed to come in waves and waves of liquid love; for I could not express it in any other way. It seemed like the very breath of God. I can recollect distinctly that it seemed to fan me, like immense wings.

"No words can express the wonderful love that was shed abroad in my heart. I wept aloud with joy and love; and I do not know but I should say, I literally bellowed out the unutterable gushings of my heart. These waves came over me, and over me, and over me, one after the other, until I recollect I cried out, 'I shall die if these waves continue to pass over me.' I said, 'Lord, I cannot bear any more;' yet I had no fear of death . . .

"When I awoke in the morning . . . instantly the baptism that I had received in the night before returned upon me in the same manner. I arose upon my knees in bed and wept aloud with joy, and remained for some time too much overwhelmed with the baptism of the Spirit to do anything but pour out my soul to God."

Charles G. Finney, *Memoirs of Rev. Charles G. Finney.*
(New York: Fleming H. Revell Co., 1876), pp. 20–23.

THE TESTIMONY OF JOHN FLETCHER

John William Fletcher (1729–1785) was of French Huguenot stock but served as the first theologian of the Methodist movement. He testified, "My dear brethren and sisters, God is here! I feel him in this place; but I would hide my face in the dust, because I have been ashamed to declare what He has done for *me*. For many years,

I have grieved His Spirit; I am deeply humbled; and He has again restored my soul. Last Wednesday evening, He spoke to me by these words. *'Reckon yourselves to be dead indeed unto sin, and alive unto God through Jesus Christ our Lord.'* I obeyed the voice of God; I now obey it and tell you all, to the praise of His love—*I am freed from sin.* Yes, I rejoice to declare it, and to be a witness to the glory of His grace, that *I am dead unto sin, and alive unto God, through Jesus Christ,* who is my Lord and King! I received this blessing four or five times before; but I lost it, by not observing the order of God, who has told us, *With the heart man believeth unto righteousness and with the mouth confession is made unto salvation.* But the enemy offered his bait, under various colors, to keep me from a public declaration of what God had wrought.

"When I first received this grace, Satan bid me to wait awhile, till I saw more of the *fruits;* I resolved to do so; but I soon began to doubt the witness, which, before, I had felt in my heart; and in a little time, I was sensing I had lost both. A second time, after receiving this salvation, I was kept from being a witness for my Lord by the suggestion, 'Thou art a public character—the eyes of all are upon thee—and if, as before, by any means thou lose the blessing, it will be a dishonor to the doctrine of *heart-holiness.*' I held my peace, and again forfeited the gift of God. At another time, I was prevailed upon to hide it by reasoning, 'How few, even of the children of God, will receive this testimony; many of them supposing that every transgression of the Adamic law is sin; and, therefore, if I profess to be *free* from sin, all these will give my profession the lie, because I am not free in their sense; I am not free from ignorance, mistakes, and various infirmities; I will, therefore, enjoy what God has wrought in me; but I will not say, '*I am perfect in love.*' Alas! I soon found again, He that hideth his *Lord's talent, and improveth it not, from that unprofitable servant shall be taken away even that he hath.*

"Now, my brethren, you see my folly. I have confessed it in your presence; and *now* I resolve before you all to confess my master. I will confess him to all the world. And I declare unto you, in the presence of God, the Holy Trinity, I am now *dead indeed unto sin.* I do not say, *I am crucified with Christ,* because some of our well-meaning brethren say, by this can only be meant gradual dying; but I profess unto you, *I am dead unto sin, and alive unto God;* and, remember, *all this is through Jesus Christ our Lord.*"

From a letter by Hester Ann Rogers, describing a meeting with John Fletcher, held in 1781; cited by Lawson, *Deeper Experiences.* Revised as: pp. 142–43.

THE TESTIMONY OF WILLIAM (BILLY) GRAHAM

Billy Graham (1918–) is an American Southern Baptist evangelist who has preached in person to more people around the world than any Protestant who has ever lived and has been instrumental in seeing more then 2.5 million people step forward at his crusades to accept Jesus Christ as their personal savior. He testified, "In my own life there have been times when I have also had the sense of being filled with the Spirit, knowing that some special strength was added for some task I was being called upon to perform.

"We sailed for England in 1954, for a crusade that was to last for three months. While on the ship, I experienced a definite sense of oppression. Satan seemed to have assembled a formidable array of his artillery against me. Not only was I oppressed, I was overtaken by a sense of depression, accompanied by a frightening feeling of inadequacy for the task that lay ahead. Almost night and day I prayed. I knew in a new way what Paul was telling us when he spoke about praying without ceasing. Then one day in a prayer meeting with my wife and colleagues, a break came. As I wept before the Lord, I was filled with deep assurance that power belonged to God and He was faithful. I had been baptized by the Spirit into the body of Christ when I was saved, but I believe God gave me a special anointing on the way to England. From that moment on I was confident that God the Holy Spirit was in control for the task that lay ahead.

"That proved true.

"Experiences of this kind had happened to me before, and they have happened to me many times since. Sometimes no tears are shed. Sometimes as I have lain awake at night the quiet assurance has come that I was being filled with the Spirit for the task that lay ahead.

"However, there have been many more occasions when I would have to say as the Apostle Paul did in 1 Cor. 2:3: 'I was with you in weakness and in fear and in much trembling.' Frequently, various members of my team have assured me that when I have had the least liberty in preaching or the greatest feeling of failure, God's power has been most evident."

Billy Graham, "The Holy Spirit," *Christian Herald* (Oct. 1978), pp. 16, 18.

THE TESTIMONY OF DWIGHT L. MOODY

Dwight Lyman Moody (1837–1899), was an American evangelist and publisher who founded the Moody Church, the Moody Bible Institute, and Moody Publishers. He testified, "The blessing came upon me suddenly like a flash of lightning. For months I had been hungering and thirsting for power in service. I had come to that point where I think I would have died if I had not got it. I remember I was walking the streets of New York. I had no more heart in the business I was about than if I had not been in the world at all. Well, one day—oh, what a day! I cannot describe it, I seldom refer to it; it is almost too sacred an experience to name—right there on the streets the power of God seemed to come upon me so wonderfully I had to ask God to stay His hand. I was filled with a sense of God's goodness, and I felt as though I could take the whole world to my heart. I took the old sermons I had preached before without any power; it was the same old truth, but there was new power. Many were impressed and converted. This happened years after I was converted myself. I would not now be placed back where I was before that blessed experience if you should give me all the world—it would be as the small dust in the balance."

Or, at another time Moody said . . .

"I can myself go back almost twelve years and remember two holy women who used to come to my meetings. It was delightful to see them there, for when I began to preach, I could tell by the expression of their faces they were praying for me. At the close of the Sabbath evening services they would say to me, 'We have been praying for you.' I said, 'Why don't you pray for the people?' They answered, 'You need power.' *I need power*, I said to myself; *why I thought I had power*. I had a large Sabbath school and the largest congregation in Chicago. There were some conversions at the time, and I was, in a sense, satisfied. But right along these two godly women kept praying for me, and their earnest talk about 'the anointing for special service' set me thinking. I asked them to come and talk with me, and we got down on our knees. They poured out their hearts, that I might receive the anointing of the Holy Ghost. And there came a great hunger into my soul. I knew not what it was. I began to cry as I never did before. The hunger increased. I really felt that I did not want to live any longer if I could not have this power for service. I kept on crying all the time that God would fill me with His Spirit. Well, one day, in the city of New York—O, what a day! I cannot describe it; I seldom refer to it; it is almost too sacred an experience to me. Paul had an experience of which he never spoke for fourteen years. I can only say, God revealed himself to me, and I had such an experience of His love that I had to ask him to stay His hand.

"I went to preaching again. The sermons were not different; I did not present any new truths, and yet hundreds were converted. I would not be placed back where I was before that blessed experience if you would give me all Glasgow. It's a sad day when the convert goes into this power for some selfish end, as for example, to gratify your ambition; you will not get it. 'No flesh,' says God, 'shall glory in my presence.' May He empty us of self and fill us with His presence."

Cited by Smith, Enduement. pp. 57–58.
From a statement made in Glasgow, Scotland,
cited by Chapman, Dwight L. Moody, pp. 412–13.

THE TESTIMONY OF PHOEBE PALMER

Phoebe Palmer (1807–1874), lay evangelist and writer, is considered the mother of the Holiness movement in the United States and the Higher Life movement in the United Kingdom. In testifying to her own experience she said of herself, "Over and over again, previous to the time mentioned, had she endeavored to give herself away in covenant to God. But she had never, till this hour, deliberately resolved on counting the cost, with the solemn intention to 'reckon herself dead *indeed* unto sin, but alive unto God through Jesus Christ our Lord' (Rom. 6:11); to account herself permanently the Lord's, and in truth no more at *her own* disposal; but *irrevocably the Lord's property*, for time and eternity. Now, in the name of the Lord Jehovah, after having deliberately 'counted the cost,' she resolved to enter into the bonds of an everlasting covenant, with the fixed purpose *to count all things but loss* for the excellency of the knowledge of Jesus, that she might know him and the power of His resurrection, by being made conformable to His death, and raised to an entire newness of life . . . On doing this, a hallowed sense of consecration took possession of her soul."

Phoebe Palmer, The Way of Holiness. Cited by Lawson.
Deeper Experiences, p. 269.

THE TESTIMONY OF EVAN ROBERTS

Evan John Roberts (1878–1951) was a leading figure of the Welsh Revival. He testified, "For thirteen years I had prayed for the Spirit; and this is the way I was led to pray. William Davies, the deacon, said one night in the society: 'Remember to be faithful. What if the Spirit descended and you were absent? Remember Thomas! What a loss he had!' I said to myself, '*I will have the Spirit*;' and through every kind of weather and in spite of all difficulties, I went to the meetings. Many times, on seeing other boys with the boats on the tide, I was tempted to turn back and join them. But, no. I said to myself *Remember your resolve*, and on I went. I went faithfully to the meetings for prayer; throughout the ten or eleven years I prayed for a revival. It was the Spirit that moved me thus to think."

[*At a certain morning meeting which Evan Roberts attended, the evangelist in one of his petitions besought that the Lord would "bend us." The Spirit seemed to say to Roberts, "That's what you need, to be bent." And thus he describes his experience:*] "I felt a living force coming into my bosom. This grew and grew, and I was almost bursting. My bosom was boiling. What boiled in me was that verse: 'God commending His love.' I fell on my knees with my arms over the seat in front of me; the tears and perspiration flowed freely. I thought blood was gushing forth." [*Certain friends approached to wipe his face. Meanwhile he was crying out, "O Lord, bend me! Bend me!" Then the glory broke.*]

"After I was bent, a wave of peace came over me, and the audience sang, 'I Hear Thy Welcome Voice.' And as they sang I thought about the bending at the Judgment Day, and I was filled with compassion for those that would have to bend on that day, and I wept.

"Henceforth, the salvation of souls became the burden of my heart. From that time I was on fire with a desire to go through all Wales, and if it were possible, I was willing to pay God for the privilege of going."

Cited by Smith, Revival, pp. 42–43.

THE TESTIMONY OF OSWALD J. SMITH

Oswald J. Smith (1889–1986) was a Canadian pastor, missions advocate, and widely read Christian author who founded The People's Church in Toronto. He testified, "It was in Tampa, Florida, February 10th, 1927. I had delivered a message on The Highest Form of Christian Service; viz., Intercessory Prayer. At the close I called for a season of prayer, and knelt where I was, beside the pulpit on the platform in the Alliance Tabernacle.

"Now I am handicapped for words. How am I going to describe it? What can I say? Nothing was farther from my mind. Not for a moment had I expected anything unusual that morning. But as the people prayed, I was conscious of an unusual Presence. God seemed to hover over the meeting. Presently the blessing began to fall. I was melted, broken, awed, my heart filled with unutterable love; and as my soul rose to meet him, the tears began to come. I could do nothing but weep and praise my precious Lord.

"It seemed as though my whole body was bathed in the Holy Ghost, until I was lost in wonder, love, and praise. I felt as though I wanted to love everybody. The world and all its troubles faded from my sight. My trials appeared, oh, so insignificant, as God, God himself filled my whole vision. Oh, it was glorious!

"The people saw it. I was conscious of their wonder as they looked up and breathed a 'Praise the Lord!' 'Hallelujah!' etc. Presently I began to pray, but only exclamations of praise and adoration poured from my lips. I saw no one save Jesus only. As I prayed the audience joined in, some in tones subdued and low, others in ejaculations of thanksgiving. All seemed conscious of God's presence and power. Tears still flowed from my eyes.

"After a while I quietly slipped out, and hurried to my room in John Monder's home. There I saw my mail for which I had been eagerly waiting, lying on the table. But it remained untouched. Back and forth I walked, my face uplifted, my heart thrilled, praising and blessing God. Oh, how near the Saviour was!

"As I continued to praise God, the door suddenly opened and a young man came in. I did not give him time to tell me what he wanted, but with quivering voice and yearning heart, I pleaded with him for Christ, and a minute later got him on his knees and poured out my heart in prayer on his behalf. It had been so easy to speak to him just then.

"After a while I stopped long enough to glance at my mail. Then, feeling that I could not bear to meet people at the dinner table, I left the house, and wandered I know not where. Every now and again as I walked along the street praising God, the tears would start to my eyes until they became so red that I wondered what the people would think was the matter with me. Time after time I was choked with unutterable outbursts of worship and love that seemed to almost overwhelm me. I sang, deep down in my soul, my own chorus:

> *Alone, dear Lord, ah yes, alone with Thee!*
> *My aching heart at rest, my spirit free;*
> *My sorrow gone, my burdens all forgotten,*
> *When far away I soar alone with Thee.*

"I seemed shut in with God. For a while as I walked I would think of something else, but in a moment my thoughts would fly back to

God, and again the tears gushed forth as my heart was melted, humbled and broken in His presence.

"At last I wended my way back to my room with a sweet, settled peace in my heart and a light that never shone on land or sea in my soul. The glow passed, but the Anointing remained. I did not speak in tongues and I never have, but I had a foretaste of what shall be hereafter. Oh, how I love and adore him! Jesus, my Lord, my God!"

Oswald J. Smith, *"The Anointing of the Spirit"*
(Toronto: The Peoples Church, n.d.).

These testimonies have been preserved for us to read primarily because they are from well-known people who took time to write their testimonies down. However, there are tens of thousands of "ordinary people" who never got their testimony in print to be preserved in a book like this. For every *preserved* testimony, there have been a thousand others given in thousands of "testimony meetings" down through the years. These testimonies from ordinary people often disappear, because the people are not well known. But there have been thousands of such testimonies given by coal miners and merchants, teachers and housewives, plumbers and masons—all ordinary people who told similar stories of God's sanctifying grace in their lives. Were these people making this up? Or did God do a work in their lives that transformed their hearts in love and granted power to love and obey Christ fully? Is such a work still available from God today?

There are thousands alive today who have experienced this work. People are more bashful in claiming it today, and fewer even have an opportunity to testify since the testimony meeting has almost disappeared. But look around you, and see who seems to live the life described in this book; then go ask them in private to tell you their story. You will hear similar testimonies from scores of ordinary people who have experienced a powerful work of love in their hearts. Listen to them talk and let their testimony raise your faith that this could happen even to you. Holiness is not just for preachers and writers and old saints—holiness is for ordinary people too!

AFTERWORD

Perhaps you have studied this book in a Sunday school class, or maybe someone handed the book to you to read. Perhaps you know all about holiness, and this book merely explained what you already believed or already received but did not know what to call it.

Or perhaps after reading this book you just don't know if you have received this work of God. What should you do? The answer is simple. Just "keep on keeping on." Holiness is not a doctrine designed to bludgeon honest believers into despair by telling them they are defective. It is a message of hope, encouragement, and possibility. It marches into your life, saying, "You can do it. You can be Christlike, you can be holy, you can live above sin . . . with God's help. The one who calls you is faithful . . . he will do it."

However, sometimes this message of optimism has the reverse effect on sincere Christians. The idea of perfect love for God and others may seem so distant a possibility that you are tempted to give up in despair. Or you come to believe that the whole teaching must be false.

Don't respond in despair or in doubt. If you are sincerely interested in the whole matter of becoming fully Christlike, keep seeking! If you are not totally convinced that living obediently is possible, keep searching. Don't close your mind on the subject. That's the trouble with many Christians when it comes to truths of the deeper life. They have "democratized" doctrine. They look around and limit their own faith for holy living to what they see in others. They don't see much holy living, so they assume holy living must not be possible. Then their doubt blocks them from ever receiving this work.

Are you interested, yet not sure you have been Spirit-baptized into the sanctified life? What should you do?

STUDY

Keep reading books, pamphlets, testimonies, magazine articles, and especially God's Word. Ask people who live exemplary lives about holiness. No one is asking you to accept a dogma without study and thinking. Use your own mind. Study the matter thoroughly so that you might become convinced of truth. Ask God, "If this is really true, show me clearly in your Word." He will be faithful.

PURSUE HOLINESS

Even if you are unclear about entire sanctification, you certainly accept God's progressive sanctification, don't you? Undoubtedly you would agree that it is God's goal to change his children into the image of his own Son—in word, thought, and action. So, follow hard after holiness. Pursue it with single-minded intensity. Become a seeker. Actively crucify the deeds of the flesh. Methodically put on thoughts, words, and actions of righteousness. Keep seeking God's power over besetting sins and powerlessness. If you seek holiness, you will find it. If you hunger and thirst for righteousness, you will be filled. People who pursue progressive sanctification inevitably come to a place of "going on" to an even deeper life.

CONTINUALLY CONSECRATE YOURSELF

Whatever you believe about entire sanctification, the Bible is clear about entire consecration: God wants all of you. God wants all your thoughts, words, actions, talents, habits, time, possessions—every part of you. What areas in your life are not now under the lordship of Jesus Christ? Practice continually bringing each of these under his full authority. Hold nothing back. As he prompts you to yield a new area to him, do so immediately, joyfully, and without resistance. Allow the Holy Spirit to fill every corner of your entire life. Resist him at no point. Give him your all. Just watch what happens!

RECEIVE THIS WORK BY FAITH

Your study, pursuit of holiness, and continual consecration will sooner or later lead you to a point of decision. It may come later; it could be soon. But when this time comes—at the moment the

Spirit convinces you of your need for full cleansing and power—surrender completely to him and reach out in faith to receive the baptism with the Holy Spirit and the work of entire sanctification. Then simply begin living the sanctified life, in God's power. How is it that you were converted? All your self-adjustment wouldn't save you. You finally had to reach out in faith and say, "Save me now."

So it is that you can say, "Fill me now," and God's sanctifying work will be done. How many times have you said, "Be gone!" to anger, jealousy, hatred, pride, impure thoughts, unholy habits, and the like? Yet, they stay on. These spirits are stronger than you are. The Holy Spirit, however, is "The Strong Man." It is he alone who can drive these inclinations from the temple of your heart. The fullness of the Holy Spirit drives out everything contrary to his Spirit, just as when the sun rises, the darkness flees. This truth is for ordinary people. It's for you. Hunger and you will be filled. Seek and you will find!

AND IF HE TARRIES—WAIT

It could be that you have completely consecrated yourself to God and had the most faith you could, yet nothing happened still. What should you do? Keep seeking. We do not know why God sometimes delays granting this work of grace in some believer's lives, but sometimes he does. It's possible that you "have done all you can," and yet God has not cleansed and filled you. Keep seeking. Don't give up and dismiss this work because you sought it for several months and nothing happened. Keep seeking. God does not always grant our request immediately. If you have placed your all on the altar and believe that God will do this—keep believing and keep seeking until he does. If you knew God might tarry a whole year would you give up this quest? Keep seeking. How about five years? Ten? How much do you hunger and thirst for righteousness? If you've done all you can, enter a period of seeking and keep seeking. What do you have to lose? Even if you sought God's sanctifying purity and power the rest of your life and never received it—would that be a wasted search?

GLOSSARY OF TERMS

Arminian. A theological position named for Jacobus Arminius that makes slight revisions to Calvinism. Arminians emphasize that humans play a role of cooperating with God in salvation and sanctification—that grace is resistible and not automatic. As applied to sanctification, Arminians thus emphasize the importance of human consecration and faith.

Atonement. The provision through the blood of Christ that saves us and sanctifies us. Both the forgiveness of sins and the cleansing from sin come only through the atonement. Salvation and sanctification are not something we achieve ourselves but come only through Christ's atonement.

Baptism of the Holy Spirit. A crisis event cleansing a believer's heart from the inner inclination to sin at entire sanctification, sometimes referred to as being filled with the Spirit. In this book, the two terms are often used interchangeably, though there is technically a difference.

Blameless. Through God's grace a Christian is not held accountable for unintended sin. He or she is held blameless, though not absolutely perfect—like a child who is immature and falls short of perfection, but the child's intention is pure.

Carnal Nature. The inclination to sin we inherit as human beings; the drive to disobey God with which we are born and which we possess even after we are saved. Sometimes confused with the flesh.

Christlike. To walk as Jesus walked in this world in word, thought, and deed. Holiness, the goal of sanctification.

Cleansing. The correction of the Christian's inner nature to disobey God. Cleansing occurs with the baptism of the Holy Spirit at entire sanctification producing holiness of life and perfect love.

Consecration. The Christian's total surrender to Jesus in absolute dedication to God, which is a prerequisite to entire sanctification.

Continual Sanctification. The work of God after entire sanctification whereby we are continually and progressively shaped to be more like Christ.

Crisis. A moment, a short time, as opposed to a process that is gradual and progressive. Entire sanctification is a crisis, though it's preceded and followed by a process of sanctification.

Depravity. The inbred sin we inherit as children of Adam, the inner nature inclining us to disobedience, or carnal nature.

Dying Out. Term to describe entire consecration or the total surrender, which is a prerequisite for entire sanctification through the baptism of the Holy Spirit.

Entire Sanctification. A crisis event for believers which occurs instantaneously—or in a short period—when a believer makes an entire consecration, reaching out in faith to receive the baptism of the Holy Spirit, which cleanses the heart from all inbred sin.

Faith. A prerequisite to being entirely sanctified, believing this work is possible and believing God has done it, we are sanctified by faith like we are saved (initial sanctification) by faith.

Filled with the Spirit. Often used synonymously with baptism of the Holy Spirit, though technically different. The filling is for use, service, power to preach the gospel and serve others; the baptism deals with cleansing the carnal nature. They often occur simultaneously, thus for the purposes of this book they are often used interchangeably.

Flesh. Human nature. Our normal human inclinations and desires, neither good nor bad, as opposed to the carnal nature, which is our inherited nature to sin.

Final Sanctification. The ultimate work making us Christlike, which occurs in glorification, so that when we see Jesus face-to-face, we shall be like him.

Full Salvation. Entire sanctification. Perfect love. Full sanctification. Salvation and sanctification are sometimes used interchangeably in this setting, though salvation is a broader term implying all that God has done and is doing to save men and women, while sanctification tends to refer to the actual practical changes in a believer's life producing greater Christlikeness which begins the moment we are saved.

Glorification. The changes God makes in a believer at death and before seeing Christ face-to-face. Also final sanctification.

Grace. Unmerited favor and changing power from God. We are saved by God's grace, and sanctified by his grace, not because we have earned it or worked for it, or in any other way deserved it. Also used to mean something more like God's undeserved power that actually changes us.

Growth. A quantitative gradual increase in the Christlikeness. Related to but different from purification, which deals with a crisis change in the quality of the Christian's nature.

Holiness. Christlikeness.

Holiness Movement. Originally a collection of individuals, associations, camp meetings, and particular local churches who considered themselves proponents of holiness within the Methodist and Methodist-related churches. Later came to define denominations including The Church of the Nazarene, The Wesleyan Church, The Free Methodist Church, The Church of Christ in Christian Union, the Salvation Army, and a host of churches in the "Conservative Holiness Movement" and still includes many local churches and pastors among The United Methodist Church.

Initial Sanctification. The actual changes in a person's thoughts, words, and deeds making that person more like Christ, which occur at and around conversion.

Instantaneous Sanctification. Entire sanctification. A momentary crisis in a believer's life when the believer is cleansed from inbred sin through the power of the baptism of the Holy Spirit and is empowered for a life of love and service, though technically can be applied to any sanctifying event when a person is actually changed such as in conversion or initial sanctification.

Intention. Related to perfection in that God can make our intention pure—with us absolutely intending to please Christ alone even though our actual performance may still fall short due to immaturity. A Christian is held blameless of unintended deeds or words.

Justification. God's legal determination of the charges against a sinner as not guilty made on the basis of the atonement of Christ and in light of our repentance and faith.

Pelagianism. A strain of theological thought named for Pelagius, a monk from Britain in the 400s, who taught that humans were not born with inbred sin and thus human nature was essentially good. Pelagianism is rejected by all orthodox Christians including Calvinists, Arminians, and Wesleyans, though the strain of thought is prevalent in modern secularism and humanism.

Pentecostal. A term relating to a second work of grace and describing most of the Holiness movement until the rise of the late twentieth century tongues movement, when holiness churches abandoned the term.

Perfect Love. A God-given power to love God with all your heart, mind, soul, and strength, and to love your neighbor as yourself, resulting in obedient living.

Perfection. Christlikeness. Absolute perfection is absolute Christlikeness; relative perfection, or "Christian perfection" is purity of intention, a heart full of nothing but a loving desire to please Christ that is enabled by entire sanctification.

Progressive Sanctification. The God-enabled gradual changes in a person's thoughts, words, and deeds making that person more like Christ as we grow toward the crisis of entire sanctification.

Purification. Cleansing from inbred sin resulting in a qualitative change, as opposed to growth, which relates to a quantitative change. Related to but different from growth, which deals with a gradual change in the quantity of Christlikeness exhibited in the Christian's life.

Sanctification. Everything that God does in us to make us more like Christ. Sanctification begins at conversion with initial sanctification, continues gradually in progressive sanctification, leads to entire sanctification, then progresses in continual sanctification until we die and through glorification receive final sanctification.

Second Blessing. A second definite work in the Christian's life following conversion which produces power over sin and power for loving service to God and others. The second blessing is entire sanctification accomplished through the baptism with the Holy Spirit, also sometimes called full salvation.

Second Work of Grace. Entire sanctification, related to the first work of grace—conversion.

Sin. Strictly speaking, a willful transgression of a known law of God—purposeful breaking of God's law; premeditated disobedience. Generally speaking, though, it is any thought, word, or deed that falls short of the absolute perfection of Christlikeness. Entire sanctification can enable a person to live above sin strictly speaking.

Suppression. The controlling, limiting, and harnessing of the carnal nature in the Christian's life, following conversion but before entire sanctification, where there is complete cleansing from this nature.

Wesleyan. A strain of theological thought named for John Wesley, the founder of the Methodists, that teaches a revised Arminianism providing for the possibility of entire sanctification or perfect love in the believer's life here and now.

Witness of the Spirit. How a believer knows for sure he or she is saved or sanctified—the Spirit witnesses to the heart a surety of the work—we "know that we know" it is done.